THE TRADER'S MINDSET

TRANSFORMING CHAOS INTO CLARITY

KODHANDA
RAMAKRISHNA VARRE
VV DURGA PRASAD VARRE

Contents

Foreword   *v*

Preface   *vii*

1. The Two Traders – Chaos Vs Clarity   1

2. Belief Is The Foundation   11

3. Visualizing Success And Discipline   18

4. Emotion Is The Enemy   30

5. Trusting The Process, Not The Outcome   48

6. The Power Of Letting Go   62

7. Shifting From Fear To Opportunity   72

8. Consistency Breeds Confidence   83

9. Manifesting Wealth Through Discipline   94

10. Mastering The Zone   104

Conclusion: The Journey to Clarity   113

Foreword

Foreword

Trading is much more than just numbers, charts, and market analysis—it is a journey of personal growth, self-mastery, and discipline. Success in trading is not just about executing the right strategies; it's about understanding and controlling the inner workings of your own mind. In fact, the real challenge often lies in overcoming fear, impatience, and emotional reactions that cloud our judgment.

This book aims to bridge the gap between market knowledge and personal mindset. Through the relatable stories of Clarity Trader and Chaos Trader, we explore the contrasting approaches that traders take in the financial markets. Chaos Trader represents the impulsive, emotional trader whose decisions are driven by fear, doubt, and the desperate need for quick gains. On the other hand, Clarity Trader demonstrates the power of discipline, patience, and belief—fundamental qualities that shape lasting success in trading.

In every chapter, you'll find lessons that go beyond just market strategies. This book dives into the mental and emotional landscape of trading, showing that the real key to consistent success is mastering the self. The principles laid out here can help transform not only your trading but also the way you approach challenges in life.

The journey from chaos to clarity doesn't happen overnight. It's a gradual process of learning to trust the system, letting go of the need for control over outcomes, and developing a mindset that can withstand the ups and downs of the market. This book is designed to be your companion on that journey, guiding you towards a balanced approach to trading where discipline and mindset go hand-in-hand with strategy.

Whether you're new to trading or a seasoned veteran, the insights shared in these pages will serve as a powerful reminder that the most important tool in your trading arsenal is your own mind. Embrace the process, learn from each experience, and trust that clarity and success will follow.

This book reflects the deep passion and understanding that we, as the authors, have cultivated over years of engaging with the financial markets. It is our hope that these insights will not only help you become a more skilled trader but will also inspire you to grow personally, developing the mental resilience that leads to long-term success in every area of life.

We invite you to take this journey with us, from chaos to clarity, and discover how mastering your mind can transform your trading experience.

Sincerely,

CMA V K Ramakrishna

VVV Durga Prasad

Preface

How to Get Maximum Benefit Out of This Book

This book is designed not just to be read, but to be *experienced*. The insights, lessons, and exercises presented within these pages are meant to help you transform your trading mindset and habits. To get the most out of this journey, here are a few tips on how to maximize the value you extract from this book:

1. Take Your Time with Each Chapter

While it may be tempting to breeze through the chapters, we encourage you to take your time with each one. Trading psychology is not a topic that can be rushed. After reading each chapter, take a moment to reflect on the stories and lessons shared. The characters of Clarity Trader and Chaos Trader represent real struggles and breakthroughs that many traders experience, and you may find parts of their journey relatable to your own.

2. Apply the Lessons to Your Own Trading Journey

This book is not just a theoretical guide; it's a practical tool. After reading each chapter, think about how the lessons apply to your own trading habits. Are you letting emotions dictate your decisions, or are you mastering your process with discipline? Use the stories to challenge your own mindset and behaviors, identifying areas where you can improve.

3. Engage Fully with the Exercises

At the end of each chapter, you will find practical exercises designed to help you internalize the concepts discussed. These exercises are an essential part of the process. Do them thoughtfully and with intention. Whether it's visualizing your ideal trading mindset, practicing emotional control, or journaling about your progress, these activities will help you build the habits needed for long-term trading success.

4. Journal Your Progress

Keep a journal as you go through this book. Write down your thoughts after each chapter, record your experiences with the exercises, and note any changes you observe in your trading behavior. Journaling will allow you to track your progress, identify patterns in your emotional and trading habits, and reinforce the lessons learned.

5. Revisit Chapters When Needed

As you progress in your trading journey, certain challenges may resurface, whether it's dealing with fear, greed, or impatience. This book is designed to be a long-term resource. When you encounter these challenges, don't hesitate to revisit relevant chapters. The lessons in this book are not meant to be learned once and forgotten, but rather practiced and refined over time.

6. Focus on Mastering Yourself, Not Just the Market

While trading strategies and market knowledge are crucial, this book focuses heavily on mastering your mindset and emotions. Always keep in mind that your greatest tool in trading is *you*. Work on mastering your thoughts, emotions, and reactions first, and the results in your trading performance will follow.

7. Adopt a Growth Mindset

As you go through the book, maintain a mindset of growth and improvement. Every trader faces ups and downs, but those who succeed are the ones who constantly seek to grow. Instead of seeing losses or challenges as failures, view them as opportunities to learn and grow. This book is a guide to help you shift from a mindset of fear and self-doubt to one of confidence and clarity.

8. Consistency is Key

The lessons in this book, particularly around discipline and emotional control, require consistent practice. Don't expect instant transformation. The traders who achieve long-term success are those who apply these principles consistently over time. Be patient with yourself, and commit to integrating these practices into your daily trading routine.

9. Trust the Process

Finally, trust the process. The book weaves together elements of belief, mindset, and discipline. It teaches that wealth and success in trading are not just about strategy but also about inner mastery. Trust that as you develop mastery over your emotions, process, and mindset, the outcomes will follow.

ONE

THE TWO TRADERS – CHAOS VS CLARITY

The world of trading is as vast and unpredictable as the ocean. Some ride its waves with balance and confidence, while others flounder, overwhelmed by its relentless currents. This chapter introduces two traders, whose journeys in the markets began at the same time, yet whose outcomes could not have been more different. One represents the chaos of undisciplined, emotional trading; the other embodies clarity, focus, and belief in the process.

The Beginning of the Journey

It all started on a cold winter morning, in the office of a local brokerage firm. Two friends, Lashwik and Durwin, both fascinated by the stock market, decided to take the plunge into the world of trading. They had read the same books, attended the same webinars, and even subscribed to the same news channels. Yet, something fundamentally different lay beneath the surface of their trading ambitions.

Lashwik, the *Chaos Trader*, was excited, but his excitement was coupled with a simmering anxiety. He approached the markets with eagerness but also a palpable sense of fear. Every time the market moved against him, his heart would race, his palms would sweat, and his mind would spiral into panic. His trades were often rushed, impulsive, and driven by a need to be constantly "in the market." He feared missing out on opportunities, and each loss sent him into a frenzy of self-doubt.

Durwin, the *Clarity Trader*, on the other hand, had a different mindset. He understood that the market was unpredictable, but instead of seeing unpredictability as a threat, he saw it as a natural part of the trading landscape. He didn't rush into trades. He waited for his setups, trusting in his strategy and, more importantly, in his ability to stay calm when things didn't go his way. Durwin believed in the process, not just the outcome. Where Lashwik saw fear, Durwin saw opportunity. Where Lashwik chased profits, Durwin focused on refining his craft.

The First Trade: A Tale of Two Mindsets

Their first day of trading would be an unforgettable one.

Lashwik was glued to the screen, his heart pounding as the opening bell rang. He had spent the entire previous night researching, convinced he had found the perfect stock to make his first big win. Without hesitation, he placed his order the moment the market opened, barely taking a breath as his order was filled. Within minutes, the stock started to dip slightly. Lashwik's confidence began to wane. His mind raced, imagining the worst-case scenario—what if the stock crashed? What if he lost everything?

As the price continued to drop, Lashwik's fear overtook him. In a panicked flurry, he sold his position, locking in a small loss. No sooner had he exited the trade than the stock reversed, surging upwards, leaving Lashwik staring at the screen in disbelief. He had sold at the exact bottom.

Meanwhile, Durwin was calm, almost serene. He had identified the same stock as Lashwik but had a different approach. While Lashwik acted the moment the market opened, Durwin took his time, allowing the stock to move and settle. He had set a limit order at a strategic point, knowing that even if the price fell momentarily, his plan accounted for it. When his order was finally executed, Durwin didn't react emotionally. He had already accepted that the market could move against him, but he trusted his analysis.

As the stock started to drop, Durwin did something remarkable: nothing. He didn't panic, he didn't sell, he didn't even check the minute-to-minute fluctuations. He simply trusted his process and stuck to his plan. By the end of the day, the stock had not only recovered but had moved higher, just as Durwin had anticipated.

Lashwik and Durwin had entered the same trade, at nearly the same time, but their results were vastly different. Lashwik had acted out of fear, while Durwin had acted out of clarity and confidence. This was the first of many lessons that would set the tone for their trading careers.

Understanding Chaos and Clarity

The difference between Lashwik and Durwin was not just their strategy but their mindset. Lashwik, the Chaos Trader, was constantly at the mercy of his emotions. He feared losing, he feared missing out, and he feared being wrong. His trades were erratic because they were driven by emotion rather than logic.

Durwin, the Clarity Trader, approached the market with a different perspective. He understood that losses were part of the game. He didn't fear them because he believed in his process. He focused on executing his strategy with discipline, knowing that over time, this would lead to success. He wasn't chasing quick wins; he was building consistency.

Chaos in trading stems from the emotional reactions to the inevitable ups and downs of the market. Traders like Lashwik allow these fluctuations to control them, constantly reacting rather than planning. They live in a state of fear, chasing profits but never finding lasting success because they lack the discipline to stick to a system. Lashwik wasn't necessarily less intelligent or less knowledgeable than Durwin. He simply lacked control over his emotions.

Clarity, on the other hand, is the product of discipline and belief. Durwin didn't need to react emotionally because he had already accepted that the market wouldn't always move in his favor. He had faith in his process, and he trusted that if he followed his plan consistently, success would come in the long run. This clarity allowed him to stay calm in the face of adversity and avoid the mistakes that plagued Lashwik.

The Lesson: Belief and Discipline in Trading

The story of Lashwik and Durwin introduces us to two crucial concepts in trading: belief and discipline. Lashwik's downfall was rooted in his lack of belief—both in himself and in his trading strategy. Every time the market moved against him, he doubted himself, which led to fear-based decisions. His trading was reactive, not proactive.

Durwin, on the other hand, had built his trading on a foundation of belief. He believed in his process, and because of that belief, he was able to maintain discipline. He didn't allow short-term losses or market fluctuations to shake his confidence. His belief kept him grounded, while his discipline ensured that he followed through on his plan, even when it was difficult.

For traders, this is a critical lesson. Success in the markets isn't just about having the right strategy—it's about having the right mindset. Without belief in yourself and your process, you'll always be at the mercy of your emotions, reacting to the market's every move. But with belief and discipline, you can stay calm, stick to your plan, and achieve consistent success over time.

As we move forward in this book, we will explore more deeply how traders like Durwin master their emotions and develop clarity in their approach to trading. We'll uncover the techniques they use to strengthen their belief and discipline, and how you, too, can transform from a Chaos Trader into a Clarity Trader.

This journey, like trading itself, is one of patience, learning, and self-discovery. But the rewards—both financial and personal—are well worth the effort.

Exercises to Practice

Now that you've been introduced to the contrasting mindsets of Lashwik and Durwin, let's work on internalizing the lessons through some practical exercises. These exercises are designed to help you evaluate your own trading mindset, build discipline, and strengthen your belief in a structured process.

Exercise 1: Emotional Awareness Journal

The first step toward clarity in trading is becoming aware of your emotional state during the process. This exercise helps you observe and document your emotions as you trade, just like Lashwik and Durwin.

Instructions:

- For your next 10 trades, keep a journal beside you.
- Before entering a trade, write down how you feel. Are you excited? Nervous? Fearful? Be honest.
- During the trade, record how you feel as the market moves—both in your Favor and against you.
- After you exit the trade, reflect on your emotions. Did fear or greed affect your decisions?

Objective:

By documenting your emotions, you'll begin to notice patterns in how your feelings affect your trading decisions. This awareness is the first step toward gaining control over your emotional reactions, just as Durwin demonstrated in the story.

Exercise 2: Create Your Trading Plan

Durwin succeeded because he had a plan and trusted his process. This exercise will help you build a trading plan that you can follow with discipline.

Instructions:

1. **Set your criteria for entering a trade:**

   - Define what conditions must be met for you to enter a trade (e.g., technical indicators, market sentiment, fundamental analysis).

2. **Determine your risk management rules:**

   - Decide how much capital you're willing to risk per trade (e.g., 1% of your account balance).
   - Set stop-loss and take-profit levels before entering any trade.

3. **Establish your emotional management rules:**

   ◦ What steps will you take to keep your emotions in check? (e.g., take deep breaths before reacting, step away from the screen during intense volatility).

4. **Write down the plan:**

   ◦ Your trading plan should be clear, concise, and something you can easily refer back to.

Objective:
This exercise ensures that you have a roadmap to follow. Like Durwin, a trader with clarity and belief in their system always has a plan to guide their decisions.

Exercise 3: Visualization and Positive Belief Practice
Durwin maintained a calm demeanour because he believed in his process and visualized success. This exercise will help you develop a similar mindset through positive belief and visualization techniques.

Instructions:

- **Visualization:** Every morning before the market opens, spend 5-10 minutes visualizing yourself trading calmly and successfully. Imagine staying calm during market volatility, sticking to your plan, and making disciplined decisions.
- **Positive Affirmations:** Write down 3-5 positive affirmations that reinforce your belief in your trading process. Examples:

   ◦ "I trust my trading plan and follow it with discipline."

- ◦ "I remain calm and focused during all market conditions."
- ◦ "Each trade is a step toward becoming a better trader."

Read these affirmations to yourself every day before you start trading.

Objective:

Visualization and positive affirmations will help you shift your mindset from fear-based, chaotic reactions to disciplined, confident decision-making.

Exercise 4: Review Your Trades with Objectivity

Durwin succeeded because he approached his trades with objectivity, while Lashwik let his emotions cloud his judgment. This exercise helps you build objectivity into your trading routine.

Instructions:

- After every trading day, review each of your trades, but do so without emotion.
- Ask yourself these questions for each trade:

  - ◦ Did I follow my trading plan?
  - ◦ Was my decision driven by logic or emotion?
  - ◦ If the trade was successful, was it because of skill or luck?
  - ◦ If the trade was unsuccessful, was it due to a flaw in the plan or emotional decision-making?

Objective:

This exercise will help you view your trades objectively, allowing you to learn from both your successes and mistakes, and improve without being emotionally affected by short-term results.

Exercise 5: The Daily Mindset Check

One of the key differences between Lashwik and Durwin was their mindset. A daily mindset check ensures that you're entering each trading session with the right approach.

Instructions:

- Before you start trading each day, ask yourself the following questions:

  - Am I feeling calm and focused?
  - Have I accepted the possibility of both winning and losing trades today?
  - Am I prepared to follow my trading plan without exception?
  - Do I trust my strategy, regardless of today's results?

Objective:

This daily check will keep you grounded and ensure that you are trading with clarity and discipline, rather than reacting emotionally like Lashwik.

Reflection Questions

After completing the exercises for this chapter, reflect on the following questions to deepen your understanding:

1. Which of Lashwik's emotional reactions do you identify with in your own trading?
2. How does Durwin's approach differ from how you currently trade?
3. What steps can you take to bring more clarity and discipline into your own trading process?

4. How do you plan to strengthen your belief in your trading strategy?

TWO
BELIEF IS THE FOUNDATION

In the world of trading, success is not just determined by the strategies you use, but by the belief that underpins those strategies. It is belief that shapes your actions, your mindset, and ultimately, your results. This chapter dives into the experiences of our two traders—Lashwik (the Chaos Trader) and Durwin (the Clarity Trader)—as they navigate the psychological challenges of trading. It will reveal how belief can either empower or cripple a trader, depending on how they harness it.

The Early Struggles: Fear vs. Belief

Durwin sat quietly at his trading desk one evening, reflecting on his journey. He hadn't always been calm and composed. In fact, in his early days of trading, Durwin was not so different from Lashwik. Fear, self-doubt, and uncertainty were his constant companions, just as they were for Lashwik now.

Years ago, Durwin, like Lashwik, had dived into the markets with excitement but quickly found himself overwhelmed. Every trade he placed felt like a gamble. The moment the market moved against him, his confidence shattered. He would question his strategy, wonder if he had made a terrible mistake, and often exit his positions prematurely—just like Lashwik had done.

But Durwin's story took a different turn the day he met his mentor, a seasoned trader named Ravi.

The Mentor's Wisdom

Durwin was at his lowest point when he crossed paths with Ravi. After a string of losses, Durwin was ready to give up on trading entirely. He believed that maybe the market wasn't for him, that success was for others—those who were smarter, luckier, or better connected. It was during this time of doubt that Ravi, a quiet but confident trader with decades of experience, offered Durwin a piece of advice that would change his life.

"Durwin," Ravi said during their first conversation, "you don't have a trading problem. You have a belief problem."

Durwin was puzzled. He had expected Ravi to critique his technical analysis or offer some secret strategy, but instead, Ravi spoke of belief. Sensing Durwin's confusion, Ravi explained further, "If you don't believe in yourself and your ability to succeed in the market, you'll never win. No strategy will save you if, deep down, you expect to fail."

Ravi introduced Durwin to a concept that would transform his trading: *the power of belief.* He explained how the law of attraction worked not just in life, but in the markets. "What you believe, you will attract," Ravi said. "If you believe the market is out to get you, you'll find proof of that in every trade. But if you believe in your ability to succeed—if you truly believe—you'll see opportunities instead of threats."

The Turning Point: Shifting from Fear to Belief

Durwin took Ravi's advice to heart. But shifting his mindset wasn't easy. For years, fear had dominated his thinking, just as it did for Lashwik now. Fear of losing money, fear of making the wrong decision, fear of looking foolish—all of it clouded his judgment and sabotaged his trades. However, Durwin was determined to change.

He started small. Every morning, before he sat down to trade, he would remind himself of Ravi's words. He wrote down affirmations that reinforced his belief in himself:

- *I believe in my trading strategy.*
- *I trust myself to make smart decisions.*
- *I attract success through discipline and confidence.*

At first, it felt strange. Durwin had never thought much about his inner beliefs before. But as the days turned into weeks, he noticed something remarkable. His approach to the markets began to shift. He no longer felt as panicked when trades moved against him. Instead of rushing to exit, he remained calm, trusting that his plan would work. His belief in his ability to succeed grew stronger with each passing day.

Lashwik's Struggles Continue

While Durwin was transforming his mindset, Lashwik remained stuck in the same cycle of fear and doubt. Every trade was a source of stress for him. His belief system was dominated by negativity:

- *The market is rigged.*
- *I'll never make it in trading.*
- *I'm just unlucky.*

These thoughts, though subtle, shaped every decision Lashwik made. When he entered a trade, he was already expecting it to go wrong. So when the market dipped even slightly, his fear would take over, and he'd exit the trade, locking in a loss. It became a self-fulfilling prophecy—what he feared most became his reality.

Lashwik's belief that the market was against him was reinforced by his experiences. He didn't realize that his mindset was attracting these outcomes. He was too caught up in his emotions to see that his lack of belief in himself was the real issue.

The Power of Belief in Trading

Ravi's teachings, rooted in the law of attraction, had a profound impact on Durwin. He began to see trading not just as a game of numbers, charts, and indicators, but as a mental and emotional practice. Belief, Ravi emphasized, was the foundation upon which everything else was built.

"If you believe you can succeed," Ravi told Durwin, "you'll approach each trade with confidence. You'll stay calm during downturns and remain patient when things don't immediately go your way. But if you believe that failure is inevitable, you'll find reasons to quit, to panic, and to blame the market."

Ravi's wisdom was more than just motivational talk—it was practical advice. Belief didn't mean ignoring the risks of the market or pretending losses wouldn't happen. It meant having faith in the process, trusting that consistency and discipline would bring long-term success, even if short-term setbacks occurred.

Belief in Action: Durwin's Breakthrough

Durwin's breakthrough came during a particularly volatile period in the market. He had placed a trade based on his analysis, but soon after, the stock started to drop. In the past, Durwin would have panicked and sold at a loss, just like Lashwik was still doing. But this time was different.

As the stock dipped lower but not hit the stop, Durwin felt the familiar tug of fear creeping in. But instead of giving in, he repeated his affirmations. He reminded himself of his belief in his strategy, his belief in the process. He stayed calm, resisting the urge to react emotionally.

Hours later, the stock reversed course and began to rise, eventually hitting Durwin's target. The trade was a success—not because of luck or timing, but because of his belief in himself and his strategy.

That day, Durwin realized that belief was not just a nice idea—it was the foundation of his trading success. Without it, even the best strategies would fail.

Belief Shapes Results

The difference between Durwin and Lashwik was clear. Durwin's success wasn't just due to his trading plan—it was his belief in that plan that made the difference. He attracted success because he believed in his ability to succeed.

Lashwik, on the other hand, was stuck in a cycle of doubt and fear. His belief system told him that the market was against him, that he would always lose, and so he did. Lashwik hadn't yet realized that his mindset was his greatest obstacle. It wasn't the market that was holding him back—it was his lack of belief in himself.

The Lesson: Belief is Critical for Trading Success

This chapter shows us that belief is the foundation of success in trading. Just as the law of attraction suggests, what you believe is what you will manifest in your life. In trading, if you believe you are destined to fail, you'll find ways to sabotage yourself, just as Lashwik did. But if you believe in your ability to succeed—if you truly internalize that belief—you'll make decisions that align with that success, just as Durwin did.

Trading is not just about strategies and numbers; it's about mindset. And at the core of that mindset is belief. The market doesn't care whether you win or lose—it's indifferent to your emotions. But your results will reflect what you believe deep down. So before you expect success, you must first believe you can achieve it.

Exercises for Developing Belief

To help you strengthen your belief in yourself and your trading process, here are some practical exercises:

Exercise 1: Affirmation Practice

Just like Durwin, start your day with affirmations that reinforce your belief in your success as a trader.

- Write down 3-5 affirmations related to your trading goals and mindset.
- Repeat them every morning before you start trading, and throughout the day when you feel doubt creeping in.

Exercise 2: Visualize Your Success

Visualization is a powerful tool in building belief. Spend 5-10 minutes each day visualizing yourself trading with calm, confidence, and success.

- Imagine yourself handling market fluctuations with ease, making disciplined decisions, and achieving your financial goals.

Exercise 3: Belief Journal

Keep a journal where you reflect on your beliefs about trading.

- After each trading day, write down any limiting beliefs or fears that arose during the session.
- Challenge those beliefs and replace them with positive, empowering thoughts.

THREE

VISUALIZING SUCCESS AND DISCIPLINE

Trading is often seen as a numbers game—a realm of charts, figures, and data. But behind every successful trader is not just a technical mastery of markets, but a mastery of their own mindset. The ability to visualize success and practice discipline in trading is as important as knowing when to buy or sell. In this chapter, we explore how Durwin (the Clarity Trader) integrates visualization and discipline into his trading process, while Lashwik (the Chaos Trader) remains trapped in a cycle of worst-case scenarios that sabotage his success.

Durwin's Approach to Visualization: Beyond Wealth

Durwin had always been fascinated by the idea of visualization. His mentor Ravi had introduced him to the power of mental imagery early in his trading career. Ravi had explained that while many traders focus on visualizing wealth—imagining themselves rich beyond their wildest dreams—true success in trading required a deeper form of visualization. It wasn't just about picturing the end result but seeing yourself master the process.

"If you only visualize the money," Ravi had said, "you're missing the point. You need to visualize the behavior that leads to the money—the calm, the discipline, the emotional control. Visualize yourself making smart decisions, not just the profits."

Durwin took this advice to heart. Every morning, before he opened his trading platform, he would sit quietly with his eyes closed and mentally run through his day. But instead of just imagining himself with more money, he visualized himself executing trades flawlessly. He pictured himself reading the charts calmly, analyzing the data without overreacting to market fluctuations, and sticking to his trading plan with unwavering discipline.

Durwin didn't visualize only winning trades—he knew that losses were part of the process. Instead, he imagined how he would react to losses, with poise and composure. He saw himself calmly accepting the outcome and moving on to the next trade without letting emotion dictate his next move.

As he visualized this calm and disciplined behavior, Durwin found that when the real trading day began, he felt more prepared. He wasn't caught off guard by sudden market changes because he had already played them out in his mind. Visualization helped him embody the very qualities that made a successful trader—not just a profitable one, but a disciplined one.

Lashwik's Descent into Fear

Meanwhile, Lashwik had a very different approach to trading. Visualization wasn't something he had ever considered important. He was focused on the numbers, the charts, and the next quick trade. But what Lashwik didn't realize was that he was visualizing—just not in the way Durwin was.

Lashwik's mind was filled with images of disaster. Whenever he placed a trade, his thoughts immediately drifted to what could go wrong. He imagined the stock plummeting, his stop loss being triggered, and his capital dwindling. Every time the market moved even slightly against him, his mind would flash worst-case scenarios, amplifying his fear.

The more Lashwik worried about losing money, the more he found himself in situations that confirmed his fears. When he entered a trade, he would become so consumed by the thought of a loss that he often exited prematurely, locking in a small loss rather than letting the trade play out according to his strategy. Over time, this pattern eroded his confidence and reinforced his negative visualization. He had unknowingly conditioned himself to expect the worst, and as a result, that's exactly what he got.

While Durwin visualized success through discipline, Lashwik was trapped in a mental loop of failure. He didn't realize that the more he imagined the market turning against him, the more he was attracting those very outcomes. His fear was becoming a self-fulfilling prophecy.

Durwin's Visuals of Discipline in Action

Durwin's visualization practice was about more than just imagining perfect trades. It was about embodying discipline—something that set him apart from Lashwik. Every time Durwin visualized his trading day, he didn't just focus on wins. He saw himself staying disciplined in the face of market volatility. He pictured himself watching the price drop below his entry point and resisting the urge to panic.

In one particular instance, Durwin had entered a trade in a stock that had recently shown strength. However, the stock began to pull back shortly after he entered. Durwin felt a familiar pang of anxiety—a feeling that every trader knows. But instead of letting it control him, he paused. He remembered the mental rehearsals he had done earlier that morning. In his visualization, he had seen this exact scenario, and in that mental picture, he had stayed calm, trusting his strategy.

Durwin took a deep breath and reminded himself that this was just part of the process. He followed his trading plan, allowing the stock room to fluctuate within his stop loss. Hours later, the stock recovered, moving in his favor, and Durwin was able to exit with a profit. It wasn't the size of the win that mattered, but how he had handled the situation with discipline. His ability to stay calm under pressure was a direct result of his visualization practice.

The Chaos of Indiscipline

Lashwik's experience, on the other hand, was a stark contrast. He had placed a similar trade around the same time as Durwin, but as soon as the market turned against him, his thoughts spiralled out of control. He saw his account balance shrinking in his mind's eye. He imagined having to explain to his family why he had lost so much money. The pressure was unbearable. Within minutes, he clicked the sell button, locking in a loss, despite the fact that the stock was still within his stop-loss range.

When the stock recovered later that day, Lashwik was filled with regret. He had exited too soon, yet again, because he couldn't control his fear. His lack of visualization—at least, positive visualization—had led him to focus on failure, and as a result, he made decisions that aligned with that fear. He had become his own worst enemy.

Visualization Beyond Profits

What set Durwin apart from Lashwik wasn't just their technical knowledge or market analysis—it was their mindset. Durwin understood that visualization wasn't just about seeing profits in his mind; it was about seeing himself behave in a disciplined manner. It was about picturing himself following his rules, staying calm under pressure, and sticking to his strategy, even when the market threw curveballs.

By visualizing discipline, Durwin had trained his mind to react calmly in real-life situations. He wasn't immune to the emotional swings of the market—no trader is—but his ability to remain composed was strengthened by his mental practice. He had built a mental image of success that was rooted not just in making money, but in how he conducted himself during trades.

Lashwik, on the other hand, had inadvertently trained his mind to expect the worst. His mental imagery was filled with panic and disaster, and as a result, he acted out those scenarios in real life. His failure to control his emotions wasn't just a lack of discipline—it was a lack of positive mental rehearsal. He didn't realize that he could have changed his outcomes simply by changing what he chose to visualize.

The Power of Mental Rehearsal

One of the most overlooked aspects of trading is the power of mental rehearsal. Durwin had realized early on that what he visualized in his mind had a direct impact on how he acted in the market. When he saw himself behaving calmly and with discipline, that mental image translated into real-world actions. By the time he sat down to trade, he had already "rehearsed" the day's challenges in his mind.

This mental rehearsal was especially important when the market was unpredictable. There were times when Durwin's trades didn't go according to plan. But because he had visualized how he would react in these situations, he was able to stay calm and execute his strategy without letting fear dictate his actions. This practice gave him an edge over traders like Lashwik, who let their emotions run the show.

Lashwik, by contrast, had no mental rehearsal. He didn't prepare himself mentally for the emotional swings of the market. Every loss felt like a personal attack, and every win was overshadowed by the fear of the next potential loss. Without any form of positive visualization, Lashwik remained reactive rather than proactive.

Visualization as a Discipline Builder

What Durwin had learned was that visualization wasn't just a tool for building confidence—it was a tool for building discipline. By imagining himself staying disciplined, he trained his mind to follow through with that discipline in the real world. It wasn't enough to just know the rules of trading; he had to see himself following those rules, even when the market was volatile.

Lashwik, on the other hand, lacked this discipline because he had never visualized it. His mind was trained to react emotionally because that's what he saw when he pictured the market. He had never taken the time to imagine himself calmly following his trading plan. As a result, when the pressure was on, he reverted to his default state—panic and poor decision-making.

Durwin's Lesson: Mastering the Process

For Durwin, the key takeaway from his journey was that success in trading wasn't just about making money—it was about mastering the process. Visualization was a critical part of that mastery. By seeing himself act with discipline, he reinforced the behaviour that led to long-term success.

In trading, the ability to control your emotions and stick to your strategy is what separates successful traders from those who burn out. Durwin understood that the real value of visualization wasn't just in imagining the money, but in imagining the process that led to that money—discipline, calmness, and emotional control.

By focusing on visualizing the process of disciplined trading, Durwin had set himself up for success. Lashwik, on the other hand, remained trapped in a cycle of emotional trading, constantly reacting to the market rather than controlling his own behaviour. Their contrasting approaches show that the power of visualization is not just in seeing the profits, but in seeing yourself follow through with disciplined actions that lead to success.

Exercises for Chapter 3

These exercises will help you practice the key concepts from Chapter 3, allowing you to build discipline and integrate visualization techniques into your trading routine.

Exercise 1: Visualization Routine for Trading

Objective: To create a daily routine of visualizing calm, disciplined trading behavior.

1. **Set aside 10 minutes each morning** before you begin trading. Find a quiet place where you won't be disturbed.
2. **Close your eyes and take five deep breaths** to relax your mind. Let go of any stress or anxiety you might be feeling about the trading day ahead.
3. **Visualize your trading day from start to finish:**

   ○ Picture yourself analyzing the markets calmly.

- See yourself following your trading strategy with discipline.
- Visualize yourself staying calm even if the market moves against your position.
- Imagine yourself accepting small losses as part of the process without emotional reaction.
- See yourself exiting winning trades confidently and not overextending.

4. **Focus on the process, not just the outcome.** Your goal is to see yourself sticking to your rules, handling any market scenario with calmness.
5. Write down any emotional triggers you noticed during the visualization. Were there moments where you felt anxious or tempted to break your rules? Reflect on how you can address those triggers in real life.

Exercise 2: Rehearse Your Trading Plan

Objective: To mentally rehearse your trading plan and build discipline.

1. **Review your trading plan** before you start the day.

   - What is your entry strategy?
   - What are your exit rules?
   - How will you manage risk?

2. **Visualize each step of your plan** as if you're trading in real time:

   - Picture yourself waiting for the right setup to enter.
   - Visualize placing a trade and watching the market move.

- See yourself executing your exit strategy, whether it's a win or a loss.

3. After each trading day, **review your actual performance** against your visualization:

   - Did you follow the plan as visualized?
   - If not, where did you stray, and why?
   - Reflect on how the visualization helped or where improvements can be made.

Exercise 3: Fear Inventory

Objective: To identify and counter negative visualizations or fears.

1. **Write down your biggest trading fears.** For example:

   - Fear of losing money.
   - Fear of missing out (FOMO) on a trade.
   - Fear of making the wrong decision.

2. **For each fear, create a positive visualization to counter it:**

   - If you fear losing money, visualize yourself calmly accepting a small loss and moving on to the next trade.
   - If you fear missing out, visualize yourself calmly waiting for a better setup, confident that opportunities will come.

3. **Spend 5 minutes daily** visualizing these positive outcomes, focusing on how you will feel and act in those

situations. Over time, this will help shift your mindset away from fear and toward calm confidence.

Exercise 4: Emotional Check-In
Objective: To develop awareness of your emotions while trading.

1. **Set a timer** for every hour during your trading day.
2. When the timer goes off, **pause for a moment and check in with your emotions**:

    ◦ How are you feeling? Anxious, confident, fearful, calm?
    ◦ Are you feeling pressure to make a quick decision?
    ◦ Are you visualizing a negative or positive outcome?

3. If you notice negative emotions or thoughts, **take a few deep breaths** and mentally return to your visualization of calm and disciplined trading.
4. **Write down your emotional state** at the end of the day. This will help you identify patterns and areas where you need to apply more focused visualization.

Exercise 5: Process-Oriented Visualization
Objective: To focus on visualizing the process of trading, not just the results.

1. **Choose a specific aspect of your trading process** that you want to improve, such as:

    ◦ Sticking to stop-loss rules.
    ◦ Waiting for the right setup.
    ◦ Staying calm during market fluctuations.

2. **Visualize yourself executing this process** perfectly:

   - If you're working on sticking to your stop-loss, imagine yourself calmly accepting a small loss without emotional reaction.
   - If you're focusing on waiting for the right setup, see yourself patiently watching the market, resisting the urge to jump in prematurely.

3. **Repeat this visualization daily** until the behavior becomes second nature. Track your progress by noting how well you execute the process during actual trading sessions.

Exercise 6: Trading Journal with Visual Cues
Objective: To track your visualizations and their impact on your trading performance.

1. **Create a trading journal** specifically for tracking your visualizations and how they influence your trading behavior.
2. **After each trading day, write down:**

   - What you visualized before the trading session.
   - How closely your actual trades aligned with your visualization.
   - Any emotional reactions during the day and how you handled them.

3. **Note any patterns** between your visualizations and your trading outcomes. Did visualizing calmness and discipline lead to better results? Did negative mental images influence your decisions?

4. **Refine your visualizations** based on your journal entries. Focus on areas where you still struggle and enhance your mental imagery to reinforce the desired behaviors.

These exercises will help you incorporate visualization and discipline into your trading routine, making them part of your daily practice. The goal is to build mental resilience and emotional control, which are essential for long-term success in the markets.

FOUR

EMOTION IS THE ENEMY

The market had been turbulent for a week, swinging between highs and lows, unsettling even the most seasoned traders. Chaos Trader, feeling the heat of his recent string of losses, sat glued to his trading desk. His mind raced, his palms were sweaty, and his heart pounded as if each tick of the market was personal. Every drop in price seemed like a direct blow, and every upward movement, no matter how slight, felt like a lifeline slipping away. He was on the edge, and he knew it.

Despite his inner turmoil, Chaos Trader couldn't help but react. His fear of losing more money and his desperate need to recover those losses gripped him with an unshakable urgency. "I can't keep losing. I need to make this back," he told himself, staring at the chart with bloodshot eyes. So, he acted. He placed more trades, larger positions, over-leveraging himself and ignoring his plan. The losses mounted, and with each loss, his resolve weakened. He spiraled further into emotional trading, trapped in a cycle of fear and impulsiveness.

On the other side of town, Clarity Trader was having a very different experience. He, too, had experienced losses that week. The market had moved against him, just as it had for Chaos Trader. But there was one key difference—Clarity Trader didn't panic. Instead of letting emotions like fear and frustration cloud his judgment, he took a deep breath and stepped away from his desk.

He made a conscious choice to review his trading journal and remind himself of the lessons he had learned: losses are part of trading. No trader, no matter how skilled, could avoid them. He opened his notebook and looked at the words his mentor had once shared with him: "Emotion is the enemy of success. The minute you let it dictate your actions, you lose."

Clarity Trader accepted his loss, knowing that his trading strategy was sound. It had been tested through both winning and losing periods. He trusted the process, not the outcome of any single trade. "I'll recover in time, as long as I stick to my plan," he reassured himself. With that mindset, he closed his laptop, took a walk, and let the market continue without him.

The following day, Chaos Trader's situation had worsened. His account balance was deep in the red. He couldn't stop replaying every trade in his mind, overanalyzing, wondering where he went wrong. The truth was, it wasn't a single trade that led to his downfall. It was the emotional decisions—overtrading, revenge trading, and ignoring his risk management rules—that had compounded his losses. His emotions had clouded his judgment, and now he was paying the price.

Clarity Trader, on the other hand, returned to his desk with a calm and composed mind. He reviewed his trades and realized that the loss he had taken the day before was not a reflection of his skills or the viability of his strategy. It was simply a statistical outcome. Sometimes, trades work out, and sometimes they don't—it's the law of probability. But it's how a trader responds to losses that defines their long-term success.

The Power of Emotional Mastery

Emotion is an inescapable part of human nature, and trading often brings out some of our most intense emotions: fear, greed, hope, and regret. However, in the realm of trading, allowing those emotions to dictate decisions can be catastrophic. Chaos Trader was the perfect example of what happens when emotions take over—panic leads to impulsive trades, and impulsive trades lead to more losses, perpetuating a vicious cycle.

But Clarity Trader understood that emotions could not be eliminated; they could only be managed. He realized that success in trading was not about being emotionless, but about acknowledging those emotions and not letting them control his actions. He didn't make decisions out of fear or greed. He acted based on logic, data, and a well-thought-out plan. This emotional mastery gave him a critical edge.

The reason most traders fail, just as Chaos Trader did, is because they are reactive. They let the market dictate their feelings and, in turn, their actions. When they experience a loss, they panic and try to recover it quickly, leading to impulsive trades. When they have a winning trade, they get greedy, hold on for too long, or increase their risk exposure beyond reasonable limits.

The Fear of Losing

One of the most destructive emotions in trading is fear. Fear can paralyze traders, making them hesitant to pull the trigger on a good setup, or it can lead them into reckless decisions, as Chaos Trader demonstrated. His fear of losing was so overpowering that it caused him to lose perspective. Instead of seeing his loss as a normal part of the process, he saw it as a personal failure—something he needed to "fix" immediately.

This fear is often rooted in a misunderstanding of what trading is. Trading is not about being right all the time. Even the best traders in the world lose a significant percentage of their trades. The key is how they manage those losses and how they respond emotionally. Clarity Trader's mentor had instilled this wisdom in him early on: losses are unavoidable, but how you react to them determines your success.

Greed—The Silent Enemy

If fear is the loud, obvious enemy, greed is the silent, creeping threat that can be just as dangerous. Greed leads traders to hold onto winning positions for too long, hoping for just a little more profit, only to see the market turn against them. It tempts them to risk more than they should, to overtrade, and to chase unrealistic returns.

Chaos Trader, after suffering from fear-based decisions, often swung to the other extreme. He would enter the market with a newfound sense of confidence, thinking, "This time I'll make it all back, and then some." But greed is just as harmful as fear because it distorts judgment, leading to irrational risk-taking.

Clarity Trader knew the balance between risk and reward. He never chased after excessive gains, nor did he let the desire for more cloud his judgment. He was content with consistent, manageable profits, knowing that over time, this approach would yield far greater results than sporadic, high-risk trades.

The Key to Consistency

What truly separated Clarity Trader from Chaos Trader was his emotional control. While Chaos Trader was constantly riding the emotional highs and lows of the market, Clarity Trader maintained a steady, disciplined approach. He understood that emotional reactions—whether driven by fear or greed—were the enemy of consistency.

Clarity Trader knew that consistency in trading came from consistency in mindset. The market is unpredictable, and no one can control it. But what traders can control is their response to the market. By mastering emotions, Clarity Trader found the clarity and discipline needed to make sound decisions, even in the most volatile market conditions.

Lesson for Traders

As a trader, emotions are your biggest enemy. While they can't be eliminated, they can and must be managed. When you find yourself in the grip of fear, step back and remind yourself that losses are part of the game. When greed starts to cloud your judgment, remember that it's better to take consistent, small profits than to chase after unrealistic gains.

The moment you allow your emotions to take control, you lose the clarity necessary to make sound trading decisions. But if you can master your emotions, just like Clarity Trader, you'll find that trading becomes less about the market's unpredictability and more about your ability to stay calm and disciplined. This, in turn, leads to long-term success.

Stop Loss: The Emotional Battle

As Chaos Trader faces a series of losses, his emotions begin to take control. One trade in particular stands out—a trade that could have been a small loss but ends up causing significant damage due to his refusal to accept the stop loss.

Chaos Trader places a trade with great optimism, convinced that the market is on the verge of turning in his favor. He sets a stop loss, but as the trade begins to move against him, he becomes fixated on the idea that the market will recover. "It's just a temporary dip," he tells himself. As the price inches closer to his stop loss, fear creeps in, but instead of letting the stop loss trigger automatically, he cancels it, hoping to avoid the loss altogether. He convinces himself that if he just holds on a little longer, the market will turn around.

But the market doesn't cooperate. The trade continues to move further into the red, and instead of a manageable, small loss, Chaos Trader finds himself facing a much larger and more painful loss. Each time the price drops, he tells himself, "I can't exit now—what if it turns around just after I sell?" The emotional grip of **hope** and **fear** keeps him in the trade far longer than any rational trader would remain.

At this point, Chaos Trader is no longer thinking about risk management or the overall health of his trading account. His entire focus is on avoiding this one loss, because in his mind, accepting the loss would feel like a personal failure. As his position continues to deteriorate, he's stuck in a vicious cycle: fear of locking in the loss and hope that the market will somehow reverse, justifying his emotional decision.

This is the trap of emotional trading—where the trader becomes emotionally attached to the outcome of a single trade, unable to step back and evaluate the situation logically. Without the discipline to adhere to his stop loss, Chaos Trader has set himself up for far greater damage than necessary.

Clarity Trader: The Power of Acceptance

In contrast, Clarity Trader approaches the same situation with a completely different mindset. He places a trade, carefully selecting a stop loss based on his analysis of the market. Before entering the trade, Clarity Trader has already accepted the possibility of losing. For him, the stop loss is not a sign of failure, but a protective mechanism—a way to ensure that any single trade won't significantly harm his overall capital.

When the market starts to move against Clarity Trader's position, he doesn't panic. He monitors the situation, but he knows that his stop loss is in place for a reason: to limit his downside and preserve his capital for the next opportunity. As the price approaches his stop loss, Clarity Trader feels no emotional attachment to the outcome. If the trade hits his stop loss, he'll exit the position, reassess, and move on to the next opportunity. He understands that not every trade will be a winner, and he's okay with that.

The market continues to fall, and Clarity Trader's stop loss is triggered. He exits the trade with a small, calculated loss. Instead of feeling frustrated or defeated, he feels satisfied that he stuck to his plan. He doesn't dwell on the loss, because he knows that trading is a probabilities game. Some trades will result in losses, but by keeping those losses small, he ensures that his capital remains intact for future trades.

The key difference between Chaos Trader and Clarity Trader is their emotional response to loss. Chaos Trader's inability to accept a loss leads him to ignore his stop loss, hoping for a recovery that never comes. Clarity Trader, on the other hand, embraces the loss as part of the trading process. By sticking to his stop loss, he keeps his emotions in check and avoids turning a small loss into a catastrophic one.

Why Stop Losses Matter

The concept of a **stop loss** is not just about limiting financial damage—it's about **psychological discipline**. A stop loss is a pre-determined point at which a trader will exit a trade if the market moves against them. The goal is to protect capital and avoid emotional decisions that could lead to devastating losses.

For many traders, the hardest part of trading is not making winning trades, but knowing when to accept a losing one. This is where **emotions like fear and hope** play a destructive role. Fear makes traders hold onto losing positions longer than they should, while hope convinces them that the market will turn around if they just give it a little more time.

Without a stop loss, trades can spiral out of control, turning manageable losses into catastrophic ones. **Chaos Trader's refusal to honor his stop loss** exemplifies this risk. By canceling his stop loss in hopes of a market reversal, he turned what could have been a small loss into a huge one. This type of emotional trading leads to unpredictable results, where losses are amplified because the trader is driven by feelings rather than logic.

Clarity Trader's approach, on the other hand, illustrates the **power of acceptance**. He knows that losses are part of trading, and he's comfortable taking a small loss if it means protecting his capital. By accepting losses gracefully and sticking to his stop loss, Clarity Trader ensures that he remains emotionally detached from the outcome of any single trade. This emotional detachment allows him to trade with clarity and consistency, while Chaos Trader remains trapped in emotional turmoil.

Lessons from Stop Loss Discipline

1. **Accept the Possibility of Loss**: Before entering any trade, accept the possibility of loss. Trading is not about winning every time, but about managing losses when they occur.

2. **Set Your Stop Loss and Stick to It**: Once you set a stop loss, treat it as non-negotiable. Cancelling or moving a stop loss to avoid a loss is a sign that emotions are in control.

3. **Detach from the Outcome**: Focus on the process, not the outcome. If your stop loss is hit, it doesn't mean you've failed—it means you've protected your capital for the next trade.

4. **Remember the Bigger Picture**: One loss won't make or break your trading career, but ignoring a stop loss can lead to significant damage. Always keep your overall trading strategy in mind.

Chaos Trader's Final Lesson

Ultimately, Chaos Trader's emotional resistance to accepting a stop loss represents one of the most common mistakes among traders. He refuses to cut his losses when the market tells him he's wrong, which leads to far greater pain in the long run. His inability to let go of his losing trade is rooted in fear—fear of losing money, fear of admitting he's wrong, and fear of failure.

Clarity Trader, on the other hand, shows that **discipline and emotional control** are key to long-term trading success. By using a stop loss consistently, he takes small losses in stride and remains emotionally balanced, allowing him to stay in the game and thrive over the long term.

Exercises for Chapter 4

These exercises are designed to help you recognize, manage, and ultimately master the emotions of fear and greed in trading. Through consistent practice, you will build emotional resilience and discipline in your trading routine.

Exercise 1: Emotional Awareness Journal

Objective: To develop awareness of your emotions during trading and recognize patterns.

1. **Create a journal specifically for tracking your emotional state** during the trading day.

   - Start by writing down how you feel before you begin trading (e.g., calm, anxious, excited).
   - After each trade, note how you felt during the trade (e.g., nervous, confident, scared, greedy) and after the outcome (e.g., relieved, frustrated, satisfied).

2. **At the end of each trading day, reflect on your emotional state:**

   - Were there any patterns? For example, did you feel more anxious during losing trades? Did greed push you to hold onto winning trades longer than necessary?
   - How did these emotions affect your decision-making?

3. **Write down one key takeaway** from each day to work on the next day. For example, "Today, I let fear prevent me from taking a good setup," or "Greed made me overtrade."
4. **Use your journal entries** to identify emotional triggers and make a plan to manage them the next time they arise.

Exercise 2: Fear Inventory

Objective: To identify the specific fears that affect your trading and neutralize them.

1. **List your top 3 fears in trading.** Common examples include:

   ◦ Fear of losing money.
   ◦ Fear of missing out on a good trade.
   ◦ Fear of making a wrong decision.

2. **For each fear, write down the worst-case scenario** if that fear came true. For example:

   ◦ Fear: Losing money.
   ◦ Worst-case scenario: I lose a certain amount, but I still have enough capital to trade another day.

3. **Create a plan for handling the worst-case scenario** if it happens. For example:

   ◦ If you lose money, how will you limit your losses? What stop-loss strategy can you use?
   ◦ If you miss out on a trade, how will you focus on finding the next opportunity without chasing?

4. **Revisit your fear inventory regularly**, especially after an emotionally charged trading session. Reflect on whether your fears are still justified or if you've gained more control over them.

Exercise 3: Managing Greed

Objective: To recognize and control greed when trading.

1. **Before each trading day, write down your profit target** and your risk limit for that day.

   - For example, "I'm aiming for a 2% return today, but I will not risk more than 1% of my capital on any single trade."

2. **As you trade, check yourself for signs of greed:**

   - Are you holding onto a winning trade for too long, hoping for even more profit?
   - Are you increasing your position size to chase larger gains?

3. **Set an alert or timer** during your trading session (e.g., every hour) to pause and ask yourself:

   - Am I following my profit targets, or am I chasing more?
   - Has greed influenced my decisions today?

4. **At the end of the day, compare your results with your original target:**

   - Did greed push you beyond your planned limits?
   - If you exceeded your target, was it through discipline, or did greed play a role?
   - If greed affected your trades, what could you have done differently?

Exercise 4: Deep Breathing and Emotional Reset
Objective: To create a technique for resetting your emotional state during stressful trading moments.

1. **When you feel overwhelmed, fearful, or greedy during a trade, stop for a moment** and take five deep breaths. Inhale slowly for 4 seconds, hold for 4 seconds, and exhale slowly for 4 seconds.

2. **While breathing, mentally repeat a calming phrase**, such as:

   - "I trust my strategy."
   - "I am calm, disciplined, and focused."
   - "Losses are part of the process; I accept them."

3. **After your breathing exercise, assess your emotional state:**

   - Has your anxiety, fear, or greed subsided?
   - Are you thinking more clearly?
   - Can you now make a rational decision based on your plan?

4. **Practice this technique daily,** even outside of trading, so it becomes second nature when you need it during stressful trading moments.

Exercise 5: The Loss Acceptance Drill
Objective: To practice accepting losses without emotional overreaction.

1. **Pick a simulated or small live trade** where you deliberately allow the trade to hit your predetermined stop-loss.

   - This exercise is not about making money but about experiencing a controlled loss.

2. **When the trade hits your stop-loss, pay attention to your emotional reaction:**

   - Do you feel frustrated or angry? Do you feel the urge to "make it back" quickly?
   - How does it feel to take a loss in a controlled manner?

3. **Write about the experience in your journal:**

   - How did it feel to take a loss calmly and according to your plan?
   - Did your emotions try to convince you to break your rules, or were you able to stay disciplined?

4. **Reflect on how this exercise can help in real trading.** The more you practice accepting losses, the less emotional impact they will have on you during actual trading sessions.

Exercise 6: Trade Plan Commitment
Objective: To build emotional discipline by sticking to a pre-determined trading plan.

1. **Before each trading session, create a clear trade plan** that includes:

   - Entry points.
   - Stop-loss levels.
   - Profit targets.

2. **Write down a commitment statement,** such as:

- ○ "Today, I will only take trades that meet my plan, no matter how tempting other opportunities may seem."
- ○ "I will accept losses as part of the process and will not make impulsive trades to recover them."

3. **During the trading session, keep your plan and commitment statement visible** so that you are reminded of your discipline.

4. **At the end of the day, reflect on how well you stuck to your plan:**

- ○ Did you make any emotional trades outside of your plan?
- ○ How did emotions like fear or greed challenge your commitment?

5. **Use this exercise daily** to strengthen your ability to follow your plan, regardless of how the market moves.

Exercise 7: Position Size and Stop Loss Relationship Exercise

- **Objective**: Understand the relationship between position size and stop loss to manage risk effectively.
- **Task**:

- ○ Choose a trade and calculate the appropriate position size using this formula:
  Position Size = (Total Capital * Risk Percentage) / Stop Loss Amount
- ○ For example, if you are willing to risk 1% of your capital (₹1,00,000) and your stop loss is ₹50, your

position size would be:
Position Size = (₹1,00,000 * 0.01) / ₹50 = 20 shares.

- **Reflection**: How does adjusting your position size based on the stop loss affect your risk management? Did you notice any changes in emotional reactions when trading smaller vs. larger positions?

Exercise 8. Visualization of Loss Acceptance

- **Objective**: Reinforce emotional detachment from losing trades.
- **Task**:

  - Sit in a quiet place and visualize placing a trade with a stop loss. In your mind, see the price moving toward your stop loss and hitting it.
  - As it hits the stop loss, visualize yourself calmly exiting the trade, accepting the loss without frustration or disappointment.
  - Repeat this exercise daily for one week, reinforcing the mindset that a small loss is just part of the process.

- **Reflection**: After practicing for a week, note any differences in how you feel about accepting losses in real trades. Does it feel easier to handle small losses when you expect and mentally prepare for them?

Exercise 9 Loss Review Exercise

- **Objective**: Analyze past trades to learn from missed stop loss opportunities.
- **Task**:

  - Review your last 10 losing trades. For each trade, check if you had set a stop loss and, if so, whether you honored it.
  - If you ignored or moved the stop loss, calculate how much you could have saved if you had exited when the stop loss was hit.

- **Reflection**: How much capital would you have preserved by sticking to your stop loss? Identify how emotions influenced your decision to stay in the losing trades longer than necessary.

Exercise 10 Real-Time Stop Loss Practice

- **Objective**: Reinforce the discipline of sticking to stop losses in live trading.
- **Task**:

  - In your next 5 live trades, commit to using a stop loss and not canceling or moving it. Each time a trade moves toward the stop loss, remind yourself of the bigger picture and trust your risk management plan.
  - Exit the trade automatically when the stop loss is triggered, even if the market begins to reverse later.

- **Reflection**: Journal your feelings and thoughts after each stop loss trade. Did letting go of the trade at the stop loss help you move on to the next opportunity with more clarity and less emotional baggage?

These exercises are designed to help you become aware of the emotions that influence your trading and develop strategies to manage them effectively. With regular practice, you'll build the emotional control necessary for long-term success in the markets.

FIVE

TRUSTING THE PROCESS, NOT THE OUTCOME

The key to mastering trading isn't about winning every trade or constantly achieving big profits—it's about sticking to a well-designed process and trusting that, over time, this process will lead to success. Traders who focus too much on short-term outcomes are more likely to become emotional and make impulsive decisions. Those who focus on the process are more likely to be calm, consistent, and ultimately successful.

The Diverging Paths of Lashwik and Durwin

Lashwik, also known as Clarity Trader, had been in the markets for a few years now. At this point, he wasn't particularly concerned with whether a single trade was profitable or not. He knew his trading system was solid—he had spent years refining it. Win or lose, his approach was the same: stick to the plan, make data-driven decisions, and trust the process.

Durwin, the Chaos Trader, was not so calm. After every loss, he would second-guess his approach. "Maybe I should try day trading," he'd think after a few swing trades didn't work out. Then, after a few missed opportunities in day trading, he'd swing back to long-term investing. His trading style was erratic, driven by short-term results, rather than trusting a process. This constant strategy switching led to inconsistent results and a growing sense of frustration.

Durwin couldn't see that it wasn't just his system that was the problem—it was his lack of trust in any system. He was focused on immediate results, jumping from strategy to strategy, and constantly worrying about whether the next trade would win. Every loss felt like a catastrophe. Every win was a temporary relief. He was emotionally tied to the outcome of each trade, and that attachment clouded his decision-making.

Lashwik, on the other hand, had learned to detach from the outcome of individual trades. He understood that no matter how perfect his system was, there would be losses. He had come to terms with the fact that trading was a long-term game. A loss didn't mean his system was flawed. It simply meant he was experiencing one of the inevitable setbacks along the way. His focus was always on executing his strategy perfectly, not on whether each trade was a winner.

Durwin's Endless Cycle of Tweaks

Durwin couldn't help himself. Every time he experienced a loss, he would immediately tweak his approach. One week, he would rely heavily on technical analysis, believing that chart patterns held the key. But after a few losses, he would suddenly switch to fundamental analysis, convinced that stock prices were driven by earnings reports and balance sheets. And then, when those trades didn't pan out as expected, he'd search for the next "holy grail" strategy—perhaps an algorithmic system or some new indicator.

His portfolio became a reflection of his frantic mindset. It wasn't consistent in terms of style or strategy—it was a patchwork of different trades, each one reacting to the last. The lack of a cohesive plan left him lost in the whirlwind of the market, always chasing short-term results but never finding stability.

Durwin's behavior was a perfect example of focusing on the outcome rather than the process. His emotions led him to seek immediate rewards, believing that if he just found the right strategy, he could eliminate losses. But in reality, his constant shifting between strategies only created more inconsistency and uncertainty.

Lashwik's Steadfast Approach

Lashwik, meanwhile, was the embodiment of discipline. He had developed a trading system based on a combination of price action, trend-following indicators, and risk management. More importantly, he trusted his system and followed it with unshakable confidence. Each trade he entered was based on a set of predefined criteria. Once in the trade, he managed his risk and never allowed emotions to dictate his actions.

When Lashwik experienced a loss, he would review the trade to see if he had followed his process correctly. If he had, there was nothing more to do—he would simply move on to the next trade. He didn't feel the need to change his system because of a loss. He knew that even the best trading systems would have losing trades. What mattered to him was that, over time, his process had proven to be profitable.

By trusting his process, Lashwik was able to stay calm even during difficult market conditions. He knew that the market could be volatile, but volatility didn't scare him—he was prepared for it. His mindset was rooted in long-term thinking. Rather than trying to win every trade, his goal was to execute each trade with discipline and consistency. He believed that if he followed his process over the long run, the results would take care of themselves.

The Law of Detachment in Trading

In *The Secret*, the law of attraction emphasizes the need for detachment from the outcome. If you're constantly obsessing over whether your goals will come to fruition, you create resistance, blocking your ability to manifest your desires. Similarly, in trading, the more you obsess over the outcome of every single trade, the more likely you are to introduce negative emotions like fear and greed into your decision-making.

Successful traders understand that they cannot control the market. What they can control is their approach—their process. The outcome of any individual trade is largely out of their hands, but by focusing on executing a solid process, they increase their chances of long-term success. When you detach from the outcome, you remove the emotional charge from your trades. You can analyze them more objectively, free from the anxiety of needing every trade to be a winner.

A Crucial Shift in Thinking

At one point, Durwin reached a breaking point. After yet another loss, he was ready to give up trading entirely. "I'm just not cut out for this," he thought. Frustrated, he called Lashwik for advice.

Lashwik, calm as ever, listened to Durwin vent. When Durwin was finished, Lashwik said, "You're focusing too much on the outcome of each trade. You can't win every time. The question isn't whether you're winning or losing—it's whether you're following your process."

"What process?" Durwin asked, confused.

"Exactly," Lashwik replied. "You don't have one. You're trying to force the market to give you wins, but that's not how it works. You need to develop a system that works for you, and then trust it. Don't change it after every loss. Stick with it."

Durwin paused. It was a simple idea, but it made sense. He had been so focused on the immediate results that he had never thought about the importance of consistency and discipline over the long term. The idea of trusting a process—rather than chasing after outcomes—was a new concept for him. But if he was going to succeed, he knew he had to embrace it.

The Mindset Shift

Durwin's mindset had been stuck in a loop of instant gratification—if a trade didn't work out, he assumed something was wrong with his approach and changed it. But the truth was, all traders face losses. Even the most successful ones. The difference between success and failure lies in how traders handle those losses.

By focusing on the process rather than the outcome, Lashwik freed himself from the emotional highs and lows of individual trades. He trusted his system, knowing that over time, it would deliver consistent results. His detachment from the outcome allowed him to trade with clarity and confidence.

Durwin, on the other hand, had to learn to let go of his obsession with immediate wins. Only then could he find the consistency he sought.

Lesson: Focus on the Process, Not the Outcome

Trusting the process is a fundamental principle in both trading and life. When you focus too much on the result—whether it's a profit or a loss—you lose sight of what's truly important: following a system that you believe in.

As a trader, you can't control the outcome of every trade, but you can control your approach. By creating a solid, well-thought-out process and sticking to it, you give yourself the best chance of success over the long term. Let go of the need to win every time, and trust that your process will lead to the results you desire.

Position Sizing: The Silent Pillar of Success

As the weeks go by, Clarity Trader's confidence in his trading system grows, but he doesn't let that confidence cause reckless behavior. No matter how promising a trade looks, he understands the importance of **position sizing**—ensuring that each trade risks a controlled, predetermined percentage of his capital. This way, even if he encounters a losing streak, his overall account remains intact, and he can continue trading without any emotional burden or financial devastation.

Clarity Trader's Approach to Position Sizing

Clarity Trader learned early in his trading journey that even the most promising-looking setups can go against him. Through his mentor's guidance, he internalized the concept that **every trade carries risk**, and no trade is guaranteed to succeed, no matter how confident he feels about it. As a result, he maintains strict position sizing rules:

1. **Risk Per Trade**: He limits his risk to a small, fixed percentage of his trading capital—usually 1% or 2%. This way, if the trade goes against him, his loss is minimal and won't harm his overall capital significantly.
2. **Consistency Over Confidence**: Even if a trade looks like a sure win, he **doesn't increase his position size** just because of his confidence. His rule is to stay consistent

with how much he risks in every trade, keeping his emotions and ego in check. No matter how tempting it is to risk more, he trusts the process that has been built for long-term success, not short-term wins.

This disciplined approach allows Clarity Trader to stay in the game over the long haul. His confidence comes not from any one trade or lucky streak but from the knowledge that his system, when followed with proper risk management, will yield positive results over time.

Chaos Trader: The Risk of Overconfidence

On the other hand, Chaos Trader's journey has taken a much different route. After a few successful trades, Chaos Trader starts feeling invincible. He begins to think, "I've finally cracked the code. I'm going to make a fortune!" He doesn't realize that his success so far has more to do with **luck** than skill or mastery.

Fueled by greed and a desire for bigger profits, Chaos Trader makes a critical error—he starts **increasing his position sizes**. Instead of maintaining his original risk limits, he places larger bets on his next trades. In his mind, doubling or tripling his position size feels like a shortcut to bigger wins. However, this strategy is deeply flawed.

One particular trade sticks out: after his third consecutive winning trade, Chaos Trader sees a setup that looks even better than the last. He's convinced this is the one that will really propel him forward. Without hesitation, he increases his position size fivefold, risking far more than his typical trade. In his mind, the risk is justified because the setup looks perfect.

Unfortunately, the market doesn't care about Chaos Trader's overconfidence. The trade moves against him, and before he realizes it, he's facing a loss much larger than he's comfortable with. Panic sets in. He doesn't have a stop loss in place, and his emotions start to control his actions. Rather than exiting the trade to minimize the damage, he **holds on** with a hope that the market will reverse and save him from his mistake. But it doesn't. Instead of a small loss, Chaos Trader now faces a devastating blow to his account balance.

The Psychology Behind Position Sizing

This chapter highlights an important psychological truth about trading: after a string of successes, novice traders often feel overconfident, leading to **reckless decisions** like increasing their position size too quickly. The desire to make quick profits can cloud judgment, leading to excessive risk-taking. This is exactly what happened to Chaos Trader.

When Chaos Trader wins a few trades, his confidence swells. Instead of sticking to his strategy, he's lured by the prospect of quick, large gains. It's natural to want to capitalize on success, but without disciplined risk management, this behavior can lead to devastating losses.

Clarity Trader understands this trap. He knows that even if his system has a high probability of success, he cannot afford to risk a large percentage of his capital on any single trade. Every time he feels tempted to risk more, he reminds himself of the long-term goal: **consistency** and **capital preservation**. His position sizing rules are his safety net, allowing him to withstand the ups and downs of the market without letting a single loss—or even a string of losses—wipe him out.

The Myth of "Feeling Certain"

One of the most dangerous beliefs a trader can have is that of certainty. Chaos Trader falls into this trap after his initial successes. He believes he's finally "figured out the market" and that certain trades are guaranteed winners. This false sense of certainty leads him to over-commit to trades, increasing his risk exposure beyond what's reasonable.

Clarity Trader, however, knows that **there's no such thing as certainty in the market**. Every trade carries risk, no matter how good it looks. By maintaining his position sizing rules, he avoids over-leveraging himself, which allows him to survive bad trades and live to trade another day.

Risking Too Much—A Common Novice Mistake

The experience of Chaos Trader is not uncommon. Many novice traders, after experiencing some early success, start **risking too much** per trade in the hope of accelerating their profits. But this strategy is a recipe for disaster. Increasing position sizes without a solid risk management plan can lead to much larger losses than anticipated, creating a downward spiral of emotional trading.

Let's say Chaos Trader started with a small risk—perhaps 2% of his account per trade. After a few wins, he's tempted to risk 10% or more per trade. The math is simple: after a couple of losses, he's down 20% or more of his account. At this point, panic takes over, and he may start taking irrational risks just to get back to where he started. This is a slippery slope, and it's how many traders blow up their accounts.

Clarity Trader avoids this trap by sticking to his position sizing rules. Whether he wins or loses, he never risks more than a predetermined percentage of his capital. Over time, this allows him to compound his gains slowly and steadily, without the dramatic swings that Chaos Trader experiences.

Conclusion: Position Sizing is the Backbone of Risk Management

Position sizing may seem like a technical detail, but it's actually one of the most important aspects of successful trading. By keeping his position sizes consistent and aligned with his risk tolerance, Clarity Trader avoids the emotional rollercoaster that Chaos Trader experiences. It allows him to trust his process without being swayed by short-term results.

For Chaos Trader, his failure to adhere to consistent position sizing—and his increasing greed—leads to larger losses that derail his progress. He learns the hard way that no trade is certain, and increasing risk when feeling overly confident is a surefire path to trouble.

Ultimately, it's not about how much you can make in one trade—it's about **staying in the game for the long run**. Trusting the process, including disciplined position sizing, is the key to doing just that.

Exercises for Chapter 5

These exercises are designed to help reinforce the lesson of trusting the process over individual outcomes and to help traders build the mindset needed for long-term success.

1. Build and Define Your Trading Process

- Write down the steps of your trading process in detail. Break it down into different phases, such as research, analysis, trade execution, risk management, and review.
- Identify any weaknesses in your process and think of ways to improve them.
- Are you following a specific set of criteria for entering and exiting trades? If not, develop a set of rules that will guide your trading decisions, such as using technical indicators, price action, or fundamental analysis.

Reflection Question:

- Are you making decisions based on a well-defined system, or are your decisions reactive and driven by emotions?

2. Review Your Last 10 Trades

- Take a detailed look at your last 10 trades. Did you follow your process for each trade, or were there moments where you deviated due to emotions or external factors?
- For each trade, note whether you followed your plan from start to finish, and what the outcome was.

Reflection Questions:

- If the trade was a loss, did you change your approach afterward?
- If it was a win, did you attribute the success to your process or to luck?
- How consistent were you in following your strategy across all the trades?

3. Practice Detaching from Outcomes

- The next time you place a trade, practice consciously detaching from the outcome. Visualize how you will feel if the trade is a loss, and remind yourself that the loss doesn't define your overall success as a trader.
- Focus entirely on executing the trade according to your rules and not on whether it results in a profit or loss. After the trade, evaluate whether you followed your process, not whether you won.

Exercise Tip:

- Write a small note or mantra you can say to yourself before entering each trade, such as: "I trust my process, not the result."

4. Create a Daily Trading Journal

- After each trading day, journal about your decisions and whether you followed your system. Reflect on how your emotions affected your actions.
- Write about any moments of self-doubt or anxiety and how they influenced your trades. This will help you track patterns of emotional trading.
- Also, track the emotional state you were in when you won or lost. Were you overly excited, anxious, or calm? How did these emotions impact your decision-making?

Reflection Questions:

- Are you letting emotions drive your decision-making?
- How do you feel after trades where you followed the process vs. trades where you acted impulsively?

5. Backtest Your Trading System

- Choose a specific timeframe and market to backtest your trading system over a series of trades.
- Record how many of your trades would have been successful if you had consistently followed your process.
- Compare this result to how many would have been successful if you had ignored your process and traded based on emotions or external news.

Reflection Questions:

- Do the results reinforce the value of following your process over time?
- How does seeing the long-term results of your system influence your confidence in sticking to it?

6. Set Long-Term Process Goals

- Instead of setting goals focused on winning a certain number of trades or earning a certain amount of money, set process-oriented goals.
- For example, aim to follow your trading rules for 20 consecutive trades, regardless of the outcome. The goal is to execute the process without deviation.
- At the end of the goal period, evaluate how closely you stuck to the process and what you learned about yourself as a trader.

Reflection Questions:

- Did focusing on the process make you feel more in control?
- Did it reduce emotional volatility during losses or wins?

7. Visualization Exercise: Focus on the Process

- Close your eyes and visualize yourself going through your trading process step by step. See yourself calmly and confidently analyzing the market, following your system, and executing trades. Picture yourself not reacting emotionally to wins or losses but instead focusing on how well you followed your plan.

- Imagine how it feels to be a disciplined trader who trusts their process. Create a mental image of yourself as this version of a trader.

Exercise Tip:

- Spend 5 minutes each morning doing this visualization exercise before you start your trading day.

8. Identify and Challenge Negative Thought Patterns

- Monitor your thoughts while trading, especially during losing trades. Write down any negative self-talk or thoughts that focus too much on outcomes, such as "I have to win this trade" or "I can't afford another loss."
- Replace those thoughts with process-focused affirmations, such as "I trust my strategy" or "Losses are part of the game, and I'm focused on the bigger picture."

Reflection Question:

- How does changing your internal dialogue affect your trading behavior and emotions?

By practicing these exercises, you will develop greater trust in your trading system, reduce emotional trading, and build the mindset needed to achieve long-term success. Remember, mastery of trading comes not from obsessing over each trade's result but from consistently following a disciplined process.

SIX

THE POWER OF LETTING GO

The Illusion of Control

Lashwik had been trading for years now, but it wasn't until his mentor, Durwin, sat him down one afternoon that he began to understand the power of letting go. Lashwik was becoming a disciplined trader, following his process and visualizing success, but there was one final lesson he hadn't yet grasped fully: detachment.

His mentor sensed this hesitation in Lashwik. "You're still too attached to every single trade," Durwin said as they sat together reviewing his latest performance. "You can't control the market, but you can control how you respond to it."

Lashwik paused for a moment, reflecting on his experiences over the past few months. Despite seeing improvements in his performance, he still found himself frustrated when trades didn't go his way. He was still fixated on winning every trade, often spending hours obsessing over charts, trying to predict the unpredictable. Durwin could see that Lashwik had not yet learned how to let go.

"You're holding on too tight," Durwin said. "And until you release that grip, the markets will continue to frustrate you."

Lashwik looked at Durwin, confused. "But I've followed the process you taught me. I've become more disciplined, but I still feel like I'm missing something. How can I let go when I have so much at stake?"

Durwin leaned forward, his voice calm but firm. "That's exactly it. You're holding onto the results too tightly. You're too focused on trying to control the outcome of every trade. Trading is about mastering yourself, not controlling the markets. The moment you try to force things, you lose. You need to let go of the need to control every outcome."

Chaos Trader's Struggle for Control

On the other side of town, Chaos Trader—let's call him Rohith—was going through a rough patch. His mind constantly raced as he tried to figure out why the markets weren't behaving the way he expected. Every night, Rohith stayed up late, charting potential movements, researching news that might move the markets, and tweaking his strategy with every new piece of information.

The problem was, no matter how much time he spent preparing, the market never acted the way he thought it would. He began doubling down on his losing trades, convinced that the market would turn in his favor if only he held on long enough. Instead, the losses kept piling up, and Rohith felt more out of control than ever.

He couldn't let go of the idea that he could predict and control the market's every move. The more he tried to force his trades to work, the more they backfired. Emotionally drained and stressed out, Rohith was stuck in a cycle of frustration and disappointment.

"I just don't get it," Rohith muttered to himself one day after another trade went against him. "I've done everything right, but nothing's working. How am I supposed to succeed if I can't even control what's happening?"

Rohith's frustration wasn't unusual. Many traders, like him, struggle with the illusion of control. They think that if they just study enough, monitor the market closely enough, or tweak their strategies frequently, they can somehow bend the market to their will. But as Rohith was beginning to learn, the market doesn't care about anyone's expectations.

Clarity Trader's Journey to Letting Go

Meanwhile, Lashwik took Durwin's advice to heart. At first, he didn't fully understand how he could let go while still being an active participant in the markets. Wasn't trading all about precision, timing, and control?

Durwin explained it further during their next meeting. "Think of trading like planting seeds in a garden," he said. "You plant the seeds, water them, and care for them, but you can't force them to grow. They'll grow when the time is right. The market is the same way. You can do all the right things—analyze, strategize, and execute your trades—but you can't force the market to move the way you want it to. You need to trust the process."

Lashwik began to shift his perspective. Instead of focusing on each individual trade as a win or lose situation, he focused on whether he had followed his process. If he did his analysis, adhered to his strategy, and executed the trade without letting emotions take over, that was a win for him—regardless of whether the trade resulted in a profit or loss.

He started journaling his trades not only for the financial outcomes but also for his emotional responses.

After every trade, he asked himself, "Did I follow my process?" If the answer was yes, then he considered the trade a success. He began to realize that, over time, the profits would come as long as he stayed disciplined.

The more Lashwik practiced letting go, the more his stress levels decreased. Instead of trying to control the market, he focused on controlling his own actions—his discipline, his emotions, and his adherence to his trading plan. It was a liberating experience.

Lessons from Detachment: Process over Perfection

Detachment doesn't mean indifference. Clarity Trader wasn't trading without care or analysis. On the contrary, he was more diligent than ever. But he understood that his role was to focus on his process—research, strategy, risk management—and not on the outcome of any single trade. He accepted that losses were part of the game, and he didn't let them shake his belief in his system.

Chaos Trader, however, was still consumed by the need to control the markets. He saw every loss as a personal failure, constantly blaming himself or the market for things not going his way. His attachment to results led him to chase losses, overtrade, and deviate from his strategy—compounding his problems.

Durwin explained that this concept of letting go didn't only apply to trading but to life itself. "The more you try to control everything, the more it slips away from you," he said. "The key is to focus on what you can control—your actions, your thoughts, your process—and let the rest unfold as it will. That's how success comes."

Applying the Power of Letting Go to Trading

Lashwik began incorporating this mindset into his trading. Instead of obsessing over every single trade, he zoomed out and looked at the bigger picture. He knew that he wouldn't win every trade, and that was okay. What mattered was that, over time, he followed his plan, learned from his mistakes, and improved his discipline.

This newfound perspective gave him a sense of peace and clarity he had never experienced before. He no longer reacted emotionally to market fluctuations. If a trade went against him, he didn't panic or double down on his position out of fear. Instead, he calmly assessed whether he had followed his rules. If he had, he accepted the loss as part of the journey.

Letting go didn't mean being passive. Lashwik was still proactive in his analysis and diligent in following his system. But he no longer tried to force things to go his way. He trusted that by consistently doing the right things, success would follow naturally.

The Transformation

As Lashwik embraced the power of letting go, his results started to improve. He wasn't making huge profits on every trade, but his losses became smaller and more manageable. His wins became more consistent because he wasn't making impulsive decisions or overtrading. Most importantly, his mental state was calm and focused, allowing him to make clear-headed decisions in the market.

Meanwhile, Rohith's results were getting worse. He was constantly reacting to market news, chasing trades, and trying to force results. His obsession with controlling the market was leading to overtrading, burnout, and stress. He hadn't yet learned that true control comes from within.

Conclusion: Trust the Flow of the Market

The market, like life, is full of uncertainty. Traders who try to control every outcome often find themselves frustrated and defeated. Those who learn to let go—focusing on their own actions rather than the uncontrollable outcomes—find clarity and long-term success.

Lashwik's journey was a testament to this. By letting go of the need for immediate gratification and trusting in his process, he unlocked the true power of trading: the freedom that comes with detachment from results. Trust the process, trust yourself, and let go of what you cannot control. Success, like the market, will flow naturally when you do.

Exercises for Chapter 6

1. Mindset Shift: Identifying Control vs. Influence

- **Objective**: Understand the difference between what you can control and what you cannot.
- **Instructions**:

  - Make a list of everything you try to control when trading (e.g., market movements, news, price fluctuations, etc.).
  - Now, make a list of what you actually can control in your trading (e.g., your emotions, your strategy, your risk management).
  - Review both lists and reflect on how much of your trading stress comes from focusing on things you cannot control.
  - Write down 3 actions you can take to focus more on what is within your control in future trades.

2. Letting Go of Outcomes Journal

- **Objective**: Track your emotional responses to outcomes and practice detachment.
- **Instructions**:

- ◦ Keep a journal for your next 10 trades. After each trade, regardless of whether it was profitable or not, answer the following questions:

  - Did I follow my process (entry, exit, risk management)?
  - How did I feel during the trade? (E.g., anxious, calm, frustrated, etc.)
  - If I experienced negative emotions, what was the cause? Was it related to the outcome or the process?
  - What can I do differently to focus more on the process next time?

- ◦ At the end of the 10 trades, review your notes and look for patterns. Did detaching from outcomes lead to clearer thinking and better results?

3. Visualization of Process Over Results

- **Objective**: Use visualization to reinforce the habit of focusing on the process.
- **Instructions**:

  - ◦ Every morning, before you begin trading, take 5 minutes to visualize your trading day.
  - ◦ Don't just visualize making money. Instead, focus on visualizing yourself executing trades with discipline:

    - You calmly analyzing the market.
    - You entering and exiting trades according to your plan.

- You accepting losses with composure and sticking to your risk management rules.

- Write down how you feel after the visualization and any new thoughts or realizations that come up.

4. Creating a Detachment Mantra

- **Objective**: Develop a personal mantra that helps you stay detached from outcomes.

- **Instructions**:

  - Write a short, powerful phrase that will remind you to let go of outcomes and focus on your process.
  - Some examples might be:

    - "I trust my process, not the market."
    - "I let go of what I cannot control."
    - "I focus on my discipline, not the results."

  - Repeat this mantra before every trade. Keep it somewhere visible while you trade (e.g., on a sticky note on your monitor).
  - Reflect after each trading day on how well the mantra helped you remain calm and detached.

5. Reframe Your Losses Exercise

- **Objective**: Change your perspective on losses and view them as part of the learning process.

- **Instructions**:

- Think back on your last 5 losing trades. Write a brief description of each.
- For each loss, answer the following:

  - Did I follow my trading plan? If not, why?
  - What did I learn from this trade?
  - How can I improve my execution on future trades based on this lesson?

- Reframe each loss as a learning opportunity, not a failure. Write down what positive takeaways you gained from these trades.

6. Focus on Process Reflection

- **Objective**: Deepen your understanding of how focusing on the process leads to long-term success.
- **Instructions**:

  - After each week of trading, reflect on your overall performance, but this time don't focus on your profit or loss.
  - Instead, write down the following:

    - How well did I follow my trading plan this week?
    - Did I let emotions influence my trades, or was I disciplined?
    - How did I feel when I detached from the outcome of my trades?

  - Celebrate the fact that you followed your process, even if you had losses. Commit to continuing to focus on process over results next week.

These exercises will reinforce the chapter's lesson of letting go of control over outcomes and focusing on mastering your own behaviour and process. Over time, these practices will help you trade with more clarity, discipline, and peace.

SEVEN

SHIFTING FROM FEAR TO OPPORTUNITY

A Loss That Shakes the Core

Lashwik sat in front of his trading screen, heart pounding in his chest. He had been here before, but never with this level of anxiety. The market had just delivered a crushing blow—a major loss that wiped out a significant portion of his account. The trade that had looked so promising just days before had taken a sharp turn for the worse. Now, instead of recovering, his mind was spiraling into a dark space of fear and self-doubt.

Lashwik had always been cautious. Early in his trading journey, he learned the importance of discipline and risk management. But this loss had caught him off guard. It wasn't just the monetary hit; it was the emotional impact that weighed heavy on him. *How could this happen?* he wondered. *What did I miss?*

The fear of losing more money began to consume him. Each time he considered entering another trade, his finger hovered over the mouse, unable to click the "Buy" button. His mind kept replaying the recent loss, amplifying his fear of failure. Soon, his trading screen, once filled with potential opportunities, became a reminder of danger and uncertainty.

Paralysis by Fear

Days passed, and Lashwik hadn't made a single trade. His fear had taken full control. Instead of analyzing the markets with the sharp, confident mindset he once had, he now avoided looking at his trading platform altogether. He didn't want to confront the market's unpredictability.

His routine had drastically changed. Mornings, which were once filled with excitement and anticipation, were now clouded with dread. He'd scroll through news feeds, forums, and trading blogs, hoping to find someone who could explain why the market had behaved the way it did. But the more he searched for answers, the more confused and fearful he became.

The paralysis Lashwik experienced was not just about money. It was about self-belief. For the first time since he began trading, he doubted whether he was cut out for the markets. *Maybe I'm just not good enough*, he thought. The weight of that doubt was suffocating.

He found himself trapped in a cycle of fear:

- **Fear of losing again** stopped him from entering new trades.
- **Fear of missing out (FOMO)** arose as he watched the markets move without him, but he couldn't act.
- **Fear of failure** loomed larger with every passing day he stayed inactive.

In his state of fear, Lashwik couldn't see any opportunity in the market. All he could see were risks and potential losses. The same setups he had confidently traded before now seemed like traps. His judgment was clouded, and fear dictated his every thought.

Durwin's Response to the Same Market

While Lashwik was paralyzed by fear, Durwin was facing the exact same market conditions. He, too, had taken a significant loss, but his approach was different. Where Lashwik saw danger, Durwin saw opportunity.

Durwin had learned long ago from his mentor that the market operates in cycles—sometimes you win, sometimes you lose, but what matters most is your ability to keep moving forward. He reminded himself that one loss didn't define him as a trader. Instead, it was a learning opportunity.

Durwin approached the market with calm, analytical precision. He didn't dwell on his recent loss. Instead, he reviewed the trade objectively:

- **What went wrong?**
- **What could he have done differently?**
- **Were there any signals he had missed, or was it just one of those times where the market didn't align with his strategy?**

With those answers in hand, he refocused on the present. Durwin knew that the market had already moved on, and so must he. He began searching for new setups, confident that opportunities still existed. His positive mindset allowed him to view the market through a lens of potential rather than fear.

Durwin wasn't reckless, nor did he ignore the risks. But instead of letting fear control him, he leaned into his discipline, relying on the same process that had brought him success in the past. He trusted that if he stuck to his plan and managed his risk, the next trade would offer an opportunity to recover.

As he scanned the charts, Durwin identified a promising setup—one that he had traded many times before. He entered the trade without hesitation, knowing that his strategy was sound. Whether this trade would result in a win or a loss was beyond his control, but what he could control was his execution.

The Mentor's Wisdom

Lashwik's fear continued to dominate him until, one day, he sought out his mentor for advice. He explained his paralysis, his fear of losing again, and his doubts about whether he could ever succeed in the markets.

The mentor listened carefully, nodding in understanding. Then he asked, *Lashwik, why are you focusing so much on your fear?*

Lashwik was taken aback. "Because I don't want to lose again. I can't afford another big loss."

That's your problem, the mentor said. *You're so focused on avoiding losses that you've forgotten why you started trading in the first place.*

He went on to explain that fear is a natural emotion in trading. But when traders focus solely on their fear, they become blind to the opportunities in front of them. *You're giving too much power to fear, Lashwik. You're letting it control your actions—or worse, your inaction.*

The mentor paused, letting his words sink in. Then he continued, *What if, instead of focusing on what could go wrong, you shifted your focus to what could go right? What if you looked at the market not as a threat, but as an endless stream of opportunities?*

Lashwik remained silent, thinking about the mentor's words. *I've been letting fear cloud my vision,* he thought. His mindset had been fixated on protecting himself from further losses, but in doing so, he had blocked himself from seeing the opportunities that still existed.

The mentor smiled. *Every loss teaches you something, but it doesn't have to define your future. Shift your perspective, and you'll see that the market is full of chances to succeed—if you're willing to look for them.*

Shifting from Fear to Opportunity

Lashwik left the conversation with a renewed sense of purpose. He realized that fear, while a powerful emotion, didn't have to be his enemy. By shifting his focus from avoiding losses to seeking opportunities, he could regain control over his trading decisions.

He made a commitment to stop dwelling on the past and to start seeing each new day as a fresh opportunity. Yes, losses would come, but they didn't have to paralyze him. The key was in his mindset: he had to trust his system and embrace the possibilities that the market offered.

Lashwik began implementing small changes to reinforce this shift in mindset:

- **Morning Visualization**: Each morning, he spent five minutes visualizing successful trades—not just profitable ones, but trades where he executed his strategy calmly and confidently.
- **Reframing Fear**: Whenever fear crept in, Lashwik reminded himself that fear was a signal, not a stop sign. It was his mind's way of urging caution, but it didn't mean he had to freeze. He could acknowledge the fear

and still act, focusing on the potential opportunity ahead.

- **Positive Self-Talk**: Instead of reinforcing negative thoughts like, *What if I lose again?*, Lashwik started using affirmations like, *I trust my process. The market is full of opportunities.*

With each passing day, Lashwik's confidence grew. The fear that had once paralyzed him was still there, but it no longer controlled his actions. He was able to trade with clarity, focusing on the opportunities that lay ahead rather than the losses behind him.

Lesson: Fear Clouds Judgment, Opportunity Clears It

The stark difference between Lashwik and Durwin's experiences highlights a crucial lesson in trading: fear clouds judgment, but shifting to an opportunity-seeking mindset clears it. When traders focus solely on avoiding losses, they become blind to the possibilities the market offers.

Fear is natural, especially after a significant loss, but it doesn't have to be debilitating. By shifting focus from what could go wrong to what could go right, traders can free themselves from the emotional chains that fear imposes. This doesn't mean taking reckless risks or ignoring danger—it means maintaining emotional balance, just as Trading in the Zone teaches.

By embracing the idea that the market is full of opportunities, traders can navigate through tough times with a sense of purpose and clarity. Fear will always be a part of the game, but how a trader responds to it determines their success.

In the same way that *The Secret* teaches the power of positive thinking, successful traders must learn to focus on opportunity rather than danger. This mindset shift allows them to see the market not as something to fear, but as a space filled with endless potential.

Exercises for Chapter 7

Exercise 1: Reframe Your Fear

Fear is a natural part of trading, but instead of letting it control your actions, you can reframe it into an opportunity for growth and learning.

Instructions:

1. **Identify Your Fear**: Write down the specific fears you have regarding your trading. For example: "I'm afraid of losing money" or "I fear the market will move against me."
2. **Analyze the Fear**: For each fear, ask yourself why you feel this way. What specific experiences or thoughts are driving this fear?
3. **Reframe the Fear**: Take each fear and turn it into a positive opportunity. Example: "I'm afraid of losing money" can be reframed as "Every trade, win or lose, is an opportunity to learn and refine my strategy."
4. **Visualize the Opportunity**: Close your eyes and visualize yourself handling the market with a focus on opportunity instead of fear. Picture yourself executing trades with confidence, regardless of the outcome.

Outcome: This exercise helps you recognize the origins of your fears and trains you to shift your mindset toward opportunity, reducing the emotional control fear has over your trading decisions.

Exercise 2: Daily Opportunity Journal

Keeping a daily journal focused on opportunities helps reinforce a positive mindset and trains you to see possibilities in the market, rather than focusing on dangers or losses.

Instructions:

1. At the end of each trading day, write down three market opportunities you saw during the day, even if you didn't act on them.
2. For each opportunity, describe how you felt about it. Were you afraid to take the trade? Did you see potential?
3. Reflect on what held you back, if anything, and how you can approach a similar opportunity in the future.
4. Write down at least one positive affirmation about your trading mindset for the day. Example: "I trust my system and know that each day brings new opportunities."

Outcome: This exercise helps shift your focus from fear and hesitation to potential and action, reinforcing a mindset of abundance rather than scarcity.

Exercise 3: Visualization for Opportunity Recognition

Visualization is a powerful tool for training your mind to focus on opportunity rather than fear. This exercise uses the technique of visualization to see positive outcomes in the market.

Instructions:

1. **Set aside 10 minutes** each morning before you begin trading.
2. Close your eyes and take a few deep breaths, calming your mind.
3. Visualize the market as a sea of opportunities. Picture yourself scanning the charts, not with a sense of dread, but with excitement about the potential that lies in front of you.

4. See yourself identifying a good trade setup. Imagine executing it with confidence, regardless of the outcome.
5. Visualize the process from start to finish—entering the trade, monitoring it without emotional attachment, and finally exiting the trade based on your system.
6. End your visualization by affirming: "The market is filled with opportunities, and I am open to seeing them."

Outcome: This daily visualization practice trains your mind to focus on the opportunities in the market, helping you build confidence and emotional resilience.

Exercise 4: Analyze Your Wins and Losses with a Focus on Opportunity

Reviewing both wins and losses is critical in trading, but it's essential to do so with a mindset that focuses on opportunities rather than mistakes or missed chances.

Instructions:

1. **Pick three recent trades**—both wins and losses.
2. For each trade, ask yourself:

   ◦ **What opportunity did I see?**
   ◦ **What could I have done differently to capitalize on that opportunity more effectively?**

3. Now, analyze how you reacted emotionally to the trade:

   ◦ Did you let fear stop you from executing the trade properly?
   ◦ Did your emotions impact how you exited the trade?

4. Reframe each loss: Instead of focusing on the monetary loss, write down what opportunities you gained in terms

of knowledge, experience, or system refinement.

5. Reframe each win: Instead of focusing on the profit, write down what opportunities your system successfully identified and how your mindset contributed to the win.

Outcome: This analysis shifts your thinking from obsessing over individual outcomes to seeing each trade as a learning experience. It helps you stay focused on opportunities, even in losses.

Exercise 5: Positive Self-Talk and Affirmations

Fear often comes from negative self-talk, which reinforces doubt. This exercise will help you develop a habit of using positive self-talk to build confidence and shift from fear to opportunity.

Instructions:

1. **Identify Negative Thoughts**: Write down any negative thoughts you've had related to your trading. For example: "I'll never get this right," or "The market is too risky."
2. **Rewrite into Positive Affirmations**: Turn each negative thought into a positive affirmation. Example: "I'll never get this right" becomes "I am constantly improving and growing as a trader."
3. **Recite Your Affirmations Daily**: Read your list of positive affirmations aloud each morning before you start trading.
4. **Create a Reminder**: Write your favorite affirmation on a sticky note or card and place it near your trading screen as a constant reminder.

Outcome: Regularly practicing positive affirmations rewires your brain to focus on opportunities and trust in your abilities, reducing the influence of fear in your trading decisions.

By consistently practicing these exercises, you can shift your mindset from fear-based trading to an opportunity-focused approach. Over time, these practices will help you develop the emotional balance necessary for consistent trading success.

EIGHT

CONSISTENCY BREEDS CONFIDENCE

The Turning Point: Consistency vs. Chaos

After months of trading, Clarity Trader started seeing a remarkable difference in his performance. What initially seemed like a slow and tedious process had now evolved into something steady and reliable. Every day, he woke up, prepared for the markets, and executed his trades according to the same set of rules. It wasn't the excitement of high profits or thrilling wins that kept him going—it was the quiet satisfaction that came from knowing he was doing things right.

On the other hand, Chaos Trader was still caught in the cycle of chasing quick wins. Some days, he experienced huge profits by jumping into high-risk trades, but the following day, he could lose it all and more. This erratic behavior led to an emotional rollercoaster. He felt a rush of excitement when things went his way, but the crushing disappointment of losses became unbearable. The constant ups and downs chipped away at his confidence, leaving him feeling unsure and desperate to regain control.

Clarity Trader's journey, however, was different. He wasn't focused on any single trade or even a single day. He understood that trading wasn't a sprint—it was a marathon. It wasn't about whether he won or lost today, but about sticking to his strategy over weeks, months, and years. With each trade, he reinforced the habits and mindset he had built: patience, discipline, and emotional control. And over time, he noticed something powerful happening—his confidence wasn't tied to the outcome of any one trade; it was tied to his behavior, his process, and his ability to stick with it no matter what the market threw at him.

The Path to Consistency

Clarity Trader's path wasn't easy, nor was it glamorous. It required daily focus, discipline, and a relentless commitment to the process. Every morning, he would review his trading plan, analyze the markets, and follow through with his strategy—whether the trades won or lost. His focus was no longer on the outcome of any individual trade but on maintaining his consistency. Over time, this consistency created a rhythm and sense of mastery that transformed his trading.

There were days when the market moved against him. Clarity Trader knew that even with a solid strategy, losses were inevitable. However, instead of reacting emotionally or trying to "fix" things, he simply accepted those losses as part of the game. He trusted that his consistent approach would yield long-term success, even if individual trades went wrong. His confidence came from this understanding—he didn't need to win every trade to be successful. He just needed to keep showing up with the same discipline day after day.

Meanwhile, Chaos Trader was still fixated on outcomes. When he made money on a trade, his confidence soared, but when he lost, his confidence plummeted. He constantly second-guessed himself, altering his strategies after every loss, hoping to stumble upon some magical formula that would give him nothing but winning trades. This erratic approach was exhausting. It wasn't long before Chaos Trader felt completely burned out, questioning whether trading was even worth it.

The Foundation of Confidence

What Chaos Trader didn't realize was that confidence in trading doesn't come from winning—it comes from consistency. True confidence is built through a process of steady, reliable actions. Clarity Trader understood this deeply. For him, confidence was rooted in knowing that no matter what happened in the market, he could count on himself to stay disciplined and follow his plan. He knew he wouldn't panic, chase losses, or make impulsive decisions. This internal confidence, built on consistency, became his greatest asset.

He also understood the importance of maintaining his routine. He didn't overcomplicate things or seek out new strategies every time something didn't go his way. Instead, he trusted that the strategy he had developed over time would eventually lead to success. This trust in his system allowed him to remain calm and composed, even when the market was volatile.

This contrast between the two traders was stark. Chaos Trader, despite his occasional wins, remained trapped in a cycle of emotional highs and lows. Each trade felt like a gamble, with no real control over the outcome. Clarity

Trader, on the other hand, felt a deep sense of peace in his trading. His confidence came from within, from knowing he could trust himself to stick to his process, regardless of whether a trade was a winner or a loser.

Small Wins, Big Results

One of the things that set Clarity Trader apart was his focus on small wins. He wasn't looking for the next big trade to make him rich overnight. Instead, he focused on small, manageable goals—improving his execution, refining his strategy, and learning from each trade. He didn't need every trade to be a home run because he understood that over time, the small wins would compound into significant results.

This approach allowed him to maintain emotional balance. He wasn't chasing after every market move, nor was he overwhelmed by losses. By focusing on the process rather than the outcome, he freed himself from the emotional ups and downs that plagued Chaos Trader. With each small win, his confidence grew—not just in his system, but in his ability to follow it.

Chaos Trader, meanwhile, was always chasing big wins. He wanted the thrill of hitting a massive profit, believing that one big trade would solve all his problems. But this approach only left him feeling more anxious and insecure. The more he chased, the more elusive those wins became. His inconsistency eroded his confidence, and over time, he began to doubt himself entirely.

The Magic of Routine

For Clarity Trader, consistency wasn't just about his trading strategy; it was about his entire approach to the markets. He developed a routine that he followed every single day. Whether the market was up or down, he started his day the same way—by reviewing his plan, analyzing potential trades, and preparing himself mentally for the day ahead. This routine became a source of stability in an unpredictable market.

Each morning, he would set aside time for quiet reflection, visualizing himself executing trades with precision and calmness. He understood that the key to long-term success was mental preparation, so he made it a daily practice. By maintaining this routine, he built a strong foundation for consistency, which in turn reinforced his confidence.

Chaos Trader, on the other hand, had no routine. His trading day was chaotic and reactive. He jumped into trades without proper preparation, and his decisions were driven by fear and greed. Without a clear routine, he felt ungrounded and overwhelmed by the market's volatility. This lack of structure only deepened his inconsistency, making it impossible for him to build true confidence.

Consistency is the Key to Success

The lesson from these two traders is clear: consistency breeds confidence. It's not about having the perfect strategy or winning every trade—it's about showing up every day with discipline, sticking to your plan, and trusting the process. Over time, this consistency creates a sense of mastery and confidence that no single trade can shake.

Clarity Trader's journey shows us that real confidence isn't something that can be gained overnight. It's built slowly, through daily commitment to disciplined actions. By focusing on the process, rather than the outcome, Clarity Trader was able to develop a deep and lasting confidence in his trading.

For Chaos Trader, the constant pursuit of quick wins and emotional trading left him feeling uncertain and frustrated. His confidence was always tied to the outcome of his latest trade, which made it fragile and fleeting. Without consistency, true confidence remained out of reach.

In the end, Clarity Trader's steady, disciplined approach allowed him to grow not only as a trader but as a person. He learned that success in trading—and in life—comes from showing up every day and doing the work, regardless of the immediate outcome. It's this commitment to consistency that builds real, unshakable confidence, leading to long-term success.

Exercises for Chapter 8:

Exercise 1: Daily Trading Routine

Goal: Develop a structured daily routine to reinforce consistency in your trading habits.

1. **Morning Preparation:**

    - Set aside 15-20 minutes every morning before market hours.
    - In a journal, write down:

        - Your trading plan for the day.
        - Any potential setups or trades you are considering.
        - A brief reflection on how you feel emotionally—are you calm, anxious, or excited?

2. **During the Trading Session:**

    - Track each trade you make, including:

        - The rationale behind the trade (why you entered).
        - Whether you followed your rules and strategy.

- Your emotional state before, during, and after the trade.

3. **End-of-Day Review:**

   - At the end of the trading day, review your trades.
   - Ask yourself:

     - Did I stick to my plan?
     - What did I do well today?
     - What can I improve upon for tomorrow?

Outcome: Over time, this consistent routine will help you build discipline and reinforce confidence in your trading habits.

Exercise 2: Focus on Small Wins

Goal: Shift focus from big wins to small, consistent improvements.

1. **Set Weekly Trading Goals:**

   - Instead of aiming for large profits, set small, process-oriented goals for the week.
   - Examples:

     - "I will stick to my stop-loss levels for all trades this week."
     - "I will enter trades only if they meet my criteria, without rushing."
     - "I will journal my emotional state before each trade."

1. **Track Progress:**

- At the end of the week, review whether you met your small goals.
- Reflect on how focusing on these small wins improved your overall confidence and trading results.

2. **Reward Small Wins:**

- Celebrate small successes, such as sticking to your rules or following your routine consistently.
- This can be a mental reward (acknowledging the achievement) or a tangible one (treating yourself).

Outcome: Focusing on small wins will help you develop consistency over time, building long-term confidence.

Exercise 3: Identify Inconsistent Patterns

Goal: Identify and correct inconsistencies in your trading behavior.

1. **Review Your Trading History:**

- Go back over your trades for the past month.
- Identify any patterns where you didn't stick to your plan or made emotional decisions.

  - Did you exit a trade too early due to fear?
  - Did you overtrade after a loss or win?

2. **Create a List of Triggers:**

- Write down specific situations or emotions that caused you to deviate from your strategy.
- Examples:

- "I got impatient waiting for the perfect entry."
- "I chased a stock after seeing it rise quickly."
- "I traded out of boredom."

3. **Action Plan for Consistency:**

   - For each trigger, create an action plan to avoid the behavior in the future.
   - Example:

     - Trigger: Exiting too early due to fear.
     - Action Plan: Set alerts to remind yourself of your target price before exiting prematurely.

Outcome: Identifying and correcting inconsistent behaviors will improve your overall trading discipline.

Exercise 4: Build Long-Term Confidence

Goal: Shift from short-term outcomes to long-term process-based confidence.

1. **Set a Long-Term Process Goal:**

   - Instead of focusing on profits, set a goal based on consistency.
   - Example: "For the next month, I will follow my trading strategy 100% without making impulsive decisions."

2. **Track Your Progress:**

   - Use a journal to note down every day you follow your process.

- ◦ Even if you have a losing day, focus on whether you stuck to your plan, not on the result.

3. **Evaluate After One Month:**

   - ◦ At the end of the month, evaluate your performance based on process, not outcome.
   - ◦ Ask yourself:

     - ▪ How consistent was I in following my strategy?
     - ▪ How did my discipline affect my confidence and emotional state?
     - ▪ Did I feel more in control of my trades?

Outcome: By focusing on long-term process goals rather than short-term wins, you will build sustainable confidence in your trading approach.

Exercise 5: Visualization for Consistency

Goal: Use visualization techniques to reinforce consistent, disciplined behavior.

1. **Morning Visualization:**

   - ◦ Each morning, spend 5-10 minutes visualizing yourself trading with discipline.
   - ◦ Picture yourself calmly entering and exiting trades according to your strategy, unaffected by emotions or market noise.

2. **Visualize Difficult Situations:**

   - ◦ Imagine scenarios where the market goes against you.

- ○ Visualize yourself responding with calmness, sticking to your plan, and accepting losses without panic or frustration.

3. **Journal Your Experience:**

   - ○ After each visualization session, write down how you felt during the exercise.
   - ○ Over time, track how this practice influences your actual behavior in real trading situations.

Outcome: Visualization will help solidify disciplined behavior in your mind, making it easier to execute consistently in real-life trading scenarios.

These exercises are designed to reinforce the key lesson from the chapter: that consistency is the foundation for true confidence. By committing to daily routines, focusing on small wins, correcting inconsistencies, and visualizing disciplined behavior, traders can build lasting confidence and long-term success.

NINE

MANIFESTING WEALTH THROUGH DISCIPLINE

The Story of Clarity Trader's Journey

Clarity Trader sat in his study one evening, reflecting on his journey. It had been years since he first started trading, and looking back, he realized that his path to wealth wasn't the straight line he once imagined. It had been filled with peaks and valleys, small victories and occasional setbacks. However, what made the difference wasn't some magical formula, a secret stock tip, or blind luck. It was something far more powerful: the combination of belief and discipline.

In his early days, he remembered being introduced to the power of belief by his mentor. "You must first believe you can succeed," his mentor had said, "before you will ever see it in your trading account." At first, Clarity Trader didn't fully understand. He had thought that success was all about the numbers, strategies, and technical analysis. And while those things certainly mattered, he soon realized that belief was the foundation upon which everything else stood.

As he grew in experience, Clarity Trader also recognized that belief alone wasn't enough. The universe might align itself with his desires, but it was still his responsibility to act with discipline. Trading required not just belief but consistent, focused action. Over time, the combination of these two—visualization and disciplined action—became the core of his approach.

Chaos Trader's Search for Instant Wealth

On the other side of town, Chaos Trader was also reflecting on his trading journey. However, his thoughts were not as peaceful. Chaos Trader was frustrated. Despite years of trying, he still hadn't found the quick path to wealth that he had hoped for. His trading account would swell with profits during good times, but just as quickly, he would see it drained after a series of reckless trades.

Chaos Trader often visualized himself as wealthy, imagining a future where he lived in luxury. But his belief in wealth never translated into lasting success. Why? Because his actions contradicted his beliefs. He wanted wealth, but his lack of discipline kept pulling him in the wrong direction. Instead of sticking to a proven strategy, he chased the next big thing, constantly jumping from one opportunity to another in the hopes of a quick win. He would visualize wealth, but when it came to his trading habits, they were disorganized and chaotic.

Chaos Trader couldn't understand why Clarity Trader was steadily building wealth while he seemed stuck in a cycle of inconsistency. Both traders had started with similar aspirations, yet their paths had diverged drastically. What Chaos Trader didn't grasp was that wealth is not simply the result of visualizing success—it must be earned through a disciplined process.

Manifestation Through Discipline: Clarity's Turning Point

Clarity Trader's turning point came when he realized that manifestation is not passive. The law of attraction is real, but it doesn't work by simply thinking of wealth and waiting for it to materialize. Manifestation, as he had learned, was an active process.

He began each day by visualizing success, but more importantly, he visualized his process—his discipline. Every morning, Clarity Trader would sit for a few minutes and picture himself following his trading plan without emotional interference. He saw himself calmly entering trades, setting stop losses, and letting go of the need for immediate gratification. He imagined the markets moving in unpredictable ways, but in his mind's eye, he didn't react with fear or greed. Instead, he remained calm and followed his rules.

This practice of visualizing disciplined action became a cornerstone of his trading routine. By mentally rehearsing his behavior in various market scenarios, Clarity Trader trained his mind to remain composed when the real trades came. He realized that wealth would follow naturally as a byproduct of his disciplined approach, not as an immediate outcome. This detachment from the need for instant results allowed him to trade without pressure, and over time, the wealth began to flow.

Chaos Trader's Struggles: The Lack of Consistency

Chaos Trader, on the other hand, couldn't stick to a routine. He often visualized himself as a wealthy man, but his trading actions were erratic. One day he would trade heavily based on a tip from a friend, the next day he would switch to a new strategy he read about online. There was no consistency, and his trading was reactive, based on the latest news or emotion.

The problem with Chaos Trader's approach was that he believed wealth was something that could be gained quickly, with the right move or the perfect trade. He didn't understand that wealth in trading is built like a house—brick by brick, trade by trade. Without a foundation of disciplined action, his wealth could never be stable. Chaos Trader's mind was filled with short-term desires, and because he wasn't willing to follow a process, his trading remained erratic.

The Lesson: Wealth Through a Process, Not an Outcome

The key difference between Clarity Trader and Chaos Trader lay in how they approached wealth. Clarity Trader understood that the manifestation of wealth was not a sprint but a marathon. It wasn't about striking it rich overnight, but rather about building wealth through consistent, disciplined actions over time.

He had learned that success in trading, like success in any area of life, was about trusting the process. Each trade wasn't about immediate profits but about following the plan he had set in place. He detached from the need to win every trade and focused on the long-term goal—building sustainable wealth.

Chaos Trader, however, was trapped in a cycle of emotional reactions. He wanted the result—the wealth—without putting in the disciplined effort. He believed in success but failed to follow through with consistent action. And because of this, he remained stuck, never quite able to manifest the wealth he desired.

Combining Visualization and Discipline: The Formula for Manifesting Wealth

The journey of Clarity Trader serves as a powerful example of how belief and discipline must work together to manifest wealth in trading. Visualization is a powerful tool, but it must be paired with action. You can't just think your way to success—you must do the work, consistently, day after day.

Wealth comes not from sporadic big wins but from disciplined actions repeated over time. The universe rewards consistency, and the markets are no different. By focusing on the process, trusting in a well-defined strategy, and letting go of the need for immediate results, traders can build real, lasting wealth.

As Clarity Trader learned, wealth is manifested through a disciplined process. And just like in The Secret, the energy you put into your trading—your belief in success, paired with consistent, focused action—will attract the wealth you desire.

Conclusion

Wealth in trading is not an outcome you chase; it's something that manifests naturally when you combine strong belief with disciplined action. By visualizing success and focusing on the process, traders like Clarity Trader can build sustainable wealth over time, while those who lack discipline—like Chaos Trader—find themselves stuck in a cycle of frustration.

Manifesting wealth is about more than just wanting it; it's about aligning your beliefs, actions, and habits in a way that attracts success. When you do this, wealth becomes not just a dream, but a reality.

Exercises for Chapter 9

1. Visualizing Your Process

- **Objective**: Train your mind to focus on disciplined trading rather than immediate outcomes.
- **Exercise**: Spend 5-10 minutes each day visualizing yourself trading in a calm and disciplined manner. Focus on the following:

  - How do you approach your trades?
  - Imagine yourself following your trading plan without deviation, even when market conditions change.
  - See yourself letting go of the outcome of each individual trade, focusing instead on executing the process with precision.
  - Picture how you feel—calm, in control, and committed to the long-term.

- **Reflection**: Write down how this visualization affects your mindset over time. Do you notice a shift in your ability to stick to your plan, even during challenging market conditions?

2. Building a Routine

- **Objective**: Establish a disciplined daily routine that supports consistent, long-term success.
- **Exercise**: Create a daily trading routine and commit to following it for at least two weeks. Include activities like:

  - **Morning visualization**: Spend 5 minutes visualizing a disciplined day of trading.
  - **Market analysis**: Dedicate time to analyzing the market, based on your strategy.

- ○ **Trading plan review**: Before entering any trade, review your trading plan to ensure the trade aligns with your long-term goals.
- ○ **Post-trade reflection**: At the end of each trading day, review your trades and reflect on how well you followed your plan.

- **Reflection**: After two weeks, evaluate your consistency. Did you stick to the routine? How did your emotions and actions in the market change?

3. Tracking the Consistency of Your Actions

- **Objective**: Measure the consistency of your disciplined behavior.
- **Exercise**: For each trade you make over the next month, use a checklist to track whether you followed your process. Include questions like:

  - ○ Did I follow my trading plan exactly?
  - ○ Did I let my emotions affect my decision-making?
  - ○ Did I enter and exit the trade based on my pre-determined criteria?
  - ○ Did I resist the temptation to make changes in reaction to market noise?

- **Reflection**: At the end of each week, tally up your scores. Review whether you were consistent in following your process. Are there patterns where you deviated? How can you improve your consistency in the coming week?

4. Long-Term Vision Board

- **Objective**: Create a visual representation of your long-term wealth goals and the disciplined actions needed to achieve them.
- **Exercise**:

  - Gather images, quotes, or symbols that represent your vision for long-term wealth and success in trading. Include both financial goals and personal growth goals, such as becoming a disciplined trader or mastering emotional control.
  - Divide the vision board into two sections:

    1. **Outcome goals**: The wealth and financial freedom you aim to achieve.
    2. **Process goals**: The disciplined habits and actions you will take to manifest that wealth.

  - Place this board somewhere visible to remind yourself daily that the process is as important as the outcome.

- **Reflection**: Revisit the board periodically. Are you aligning your daily actions with the process that will help you achieve your long-term goals?

5. Detach from Immediate Results Challenge

- **Objective**: Practice detachment from the outcome of individual trades.
- **Exercise**: Over the next month, track how well you can detach emotionally from individual trades. Set an intention at the beginning of each trading day to focus solely on executing your process, without worrying

about whether a trade results in a win or loss.

- At the end of the day, rate yourself on a scale of 1 to 10 based on how well you detached from the outcome of each trade.
- If you find yourself overly focused on the result of a trade, stop and remind yourself that wealth is built through consistency, not one trade.

- **Reflection**: At the end of the month, assess how your mindset has changed. Are you less stressed about individual trades? Has your focus shifted more towards the long-term?

6. Weekly Manifestation Reflection

- **Objective**: Develop a weekly habit of reflecting on how your beliefs and actions are aligned with your trading goals.
- **Exercise**:

  - At the end of each week, spend 10 minutes journaling about the following:

    - Did you believe in your ability to succeed this week?
    - How well did you stick to your trading process?
    - Were there any moments where you let emotions like fear or greed dictate your actions?
    - How did your actions this week contribute to your long-term vision of wealth?

- **Reflection**: As you journal week by week, notice any patterns. Is your belief in your ability growing? Are you becoming more disciplined? Use this reflection time to make adjustments and strengthen your approach.

These exercises will help solidify the concepts of combining belief with disciplined action, encouraging long-term consistency and focus on manifesting wealth through a solid trading process.

TEN

MASTERING THE ZONE

Clarity Trader, after months and years of consistent discipline, focus, and belief in his process, had reached a point that few traders ever do. Every morning, as he sat down at his trading desk, there was no tension, no fear, no nervousness. He wasn't obsessively checking the news or worrying about the latest economic reports. He was calm, collected, and confident. Every trade he made felt natural—almost effortless. He was in what athletes and artists call "the zone," where everything flows with a rhythm that feels second nature.

It wasn't that Clarity Trader never experienced losses anymore; losses were a natural part of the game. But his relationship with them had changed. There was no longer the fear that once gripped him, or the rush of euphoria after a big win. His emotions were steady, like a river flowing smoothly no matter what the conditions were. Every trade was made not with hesitation, but with a deep sense of trust—trust in himself, his process, and the market.

In contrast, Chaos Trader, despite having been in the markets for just as long, was still struggling. He was still caught in the emotional turbulence that came with each market move. A win would send him into a state of temporary elation, followed by anxiety about whether he could replicate that success. A loss would spiral him into self-doubt, leading to impulsive trades and erratic decisions. Chaos Trader was far from "the zone." His mind was cluttered with doubt, fear, and the constant need for control over every trade.

The Journey to the Zone

Clarity Trader's journey to mastery was not an overnight success. It had taken years of refining his mindset, battling emotions, and developing unshakable confidence in his process. He remembered the early days when he had been like Chaos Trader—worried about every fluctuation in the market, gripped by fear during downturns, and euphoric during rallies. But over time, he learned the true essence of trading: it wasn't about winning every trade, nor was it about always being right. It was about becoming attuned to the market, understanding that it had its own rhythm, its own flow, and learning how to move with it rather than fight against it.

His mentor had taught him a valuable lesson early on: "The market doesn't care about your emotions. It simply moves. The only thing you control is your actions, and when those actions come from a place of calm, focused clarity, that's when you enter the zone."

The Flow of Effortless Trading

For Clarity Trader, being in the zone wasn't about luck or chance; it was the culmination of all his hard work. His daily routine was the foundation. He would wake up early, meditate for 10 minutes to clear his mind, then spend some time reviewing his trading plan. Before even opening his charts, he would visualize himself trading with discipline, following his system without hesitation.

When he finally sat down to trade, it wasn't with the mindset of "I must win today." It was with the mindset of "I will follow my process, no matter what." This shift in thinking was what allowed him to stay detached from the outcome of each individual trade. He wasn't chasing profits; he was executing a well-thought-out plan, knowing that over time, the plan would yield results.

Each trade, for Clarity Trader, was just another step in a long journey. He didn't celebrate a win too much, nor did he mourn a loss. He simply moved on, focused on the next opportunity. His confidence didn't come from his recent performance but from his unwavering trust in his system.

Chaos Trader's Struggle

Meanwhile, Chaos Trader remained trapped in the endless cycle of emotional highs and lows. After a string of losses, he would try to "get even" by making larger, riskier trades. When those inevitably didn't work out, his confidence would crumble, and he would retreat into inaction, paralyzed by the fear of losing more money.

What Chaos Trader didn't realize was that his emotional reactions to the market were what kept him from finding success. Instead of focusing on mastering his process, he was focused on controlling outcomes. And in a market as unpredictable as the stock market, trying to control every outcome is a recipe for disaster.

Chaos Trader's belief system was also working against him. Deep down, he didn't truly believe that he could succeed long term. Every loss felt like a confirmation of his doubts, and every win felt like a fluke, something that wouldn't last. This lack of belief in himself was why he couldn't reach the zone. Without that foundation of confidence, his trading decisions were always reactive, driven by emotion rather than logic.

What It Means to Master the Zone

To master the zone in trading means to operate from a place of deep focus, where the mind is no longer caught up in fear, greed, or doubt. In this state, the trader is fully present, responding to the market not with impulse but with calm, calculated action. It's about being in harmony with the market rather than trying to dominate or outsmart it.

For Clarity Trader, this mastery came from a combination of factors:

- **Mental Discipline**: He had trained his mind to stay calm in all market conditions. This mental discipline allowed him to make rational decisions rather than emotional ones.
- **Confidence in His System**: Clarity Trader trusted his process. He had built a system that worked for him and, more importantly, he had the patience to stick with it, even when it didn't produce immediate results.
- **Emotional Detachment**: By detaching from the outcome of each trade, Clarity Trader freed himself from the emotional swings that plagued most traders. His goal wasn't to win every trade, but to trade consistently over the long term.
- **Flow State**: The zone was the result of this mental, emotional, and physical alignment. When everything flowed together—his mindset, his discipline, and his actions—he entered a state of effortless trading.

The Challenge of Entering the Zone

Reaching the zone isn't easy, and it's not a permanent state. Even Clarity Trader had days when he felt himself slipping back into old habits—checking the news too often, worrying about a trade's outcome, or feeling the sting of a loss. But the difference was that he recognized these feelings for what they were: distractions from his true purpose.

Chaos Trader, on the other hand, didn't even realize that the zone existed. To him, trading was a constant battle of trying to predict the market's next move, and every trade was a matter of survival. He was too focused on short-term results to see the bigger picture—that trading was a marathon, not a sprint.

The Path to Mastery

Mastering the zone requires a shift in mindset. It's about letting go of the need for control, embracing the process, and trusting that with consistent effort, the results will come. Clarity Trader knew that true mastery wasn't about winning every trade—it was about becoming the kind of trader who could stay calm and focused, no matter what the market threw at him.

By following his process, visualizing success, and letting go of emotional attachment to outcomes, Clarity Trader had finally mastered the art of trading. He had entered the zone, and from there, trading became not just a way to make money, but a craft he had truly mastered.

Exercises for Chapter 10

These exercises are designed to help you practice the concepts discussed in this chapter, enabling you to build the mindset and discipline necessary to enter the trading zone.

1. Meditation for Mental Clarity

One of the key elements of being in "the zone" is mental clarity. Meditation can help you achieve this by training your mind to stay present and focused.

- **Exercise**: Dedicate at least 10 minutes every day to mindfulness meditation.

  - Sit in a quiet place, close your eyes, and focus on your breathing.
  - If your mind starts to wander, gently bring your attention back to your breath.
  - After the session, note how you feel. The goal is to gradually improve your ability to stay present and calm, which will help you in high-pressure trading situations.

2. Daily Trading Visualization

Visualization is a powerful tool for reinforcing positive behaviors. In this exercise, you'll visualize yourself trading calmly, with discipline and focus.

- **Exercise**: Before the market opens, take 5 minutes to close your eyes and visualize a trading day where you follow your strategy flawlessly.

  - Imagine yourself making decisions without hesitation, based solely on your system.
  - Visualize yourself taking a loss calmly, knowing that it's part of the process, and moving on to the next trade without emotional attachment.
  - After each trading day, reflect on how close your actual behavior was to the ideal day you visualized.

3. Journaling for Emotional Awareness

Becoming aware of your emotions during trading is crucial to mastering the zone. Keeping a trading journal can help you identify emotional patterns that may be affecting your decisions.

- **Exercise**: After each trading day, write down:

  - The trades you made.
  - The emotions you felt during each trade—whether it was fear, greed, excitement, or frustration.
  - How those emotions affected your decision-making.
  - Your plan for handling those emotions better next time (e.g., taking a deep breath, stepping away from the screen).

Over time, this practice will help you recognize emotional triggers and develop strategies to manage them more effectively.

4. Process vs. Outcome Reflection

Mastering the zone involves focusing on the process rather than the outcome of each trade. This exercise helps you shift your mindset from short-term results to long-term consistency.

- **Exercise**: At the end of each week, review your trades and assess them based on your adherence to your process rather than the profits or losses you made.

  - Did you follow your rules?
  - Did you trade according to your plan?
  - Were your decisions based on your strategy, not emotions?

Write down the lessons you learned and how you can improve your process next week. The goal is to measure success by how well you followed your plan, not by how much money you made.

5. Set Up a Routine for Entering the Zone

Creating a daily routine helps you get into the right mindset for trading.

- **Exercise**: Design a pre-trading routine that helps you achieve a calm, focused state before you start trading each day. This could include:

  - Reviewing your trading plan.
  - Checking market conditions without making emotional judgments.
  - Meditating or practicing deep breathing for a few minutes.
  - Visualizing your ideal trading day, where you follow your strategy with discipline.

Implement this routine every day, and adjust it as necessary until it becomes a natural part of your trading process.

6. Recognizing the Zone

Learning to recognize when you're in the zone and when you're not is essential for improvement.

- **Exercise**: Throughout the trading day, practice identifying when you're in the zone:

  - When you feel calm, focused, and unattached to the outcome, note it down.

- Conversely, when you notice yourself becoming emotional or overly reactive, take a mental note.
- Step away from the screen if you feel emotions starting to take over, and come back when you're calm.

The more you recognize these states, the easier it will be to correct course and maintain the zone throughout your trading day.

7. Accountability Partner

Having someone to hold you accountable can reinforce discipline.

- **Exercise**: Find a trading partner or mentor to review your trades with on a weekly basis.

  - Share your trading journal with them, including your emotional reflections and adherence to your process.
  - Ask them for feedback on where you can improve in terms of mindset, discipline, and emotional control.
  - Set goals together for the next week, focusing on process-based improvements rather than specific trade outcomes.

These exercises are intended to help you build the habits and mindset necessary to master the zone. As you practice them consistently, you'll find yourself becoming more detached from individual outcomes and more aligned with the discipline required for long-term success.

Conclusion: The Journey To Clarity

The journey of trading is not unlike the journey of life—filled with twists, turns, highs, and lows. For those who dare to embark on this path, the challenges can often seem insurmountable. But as we have seen through the lives of two traders, the difference between chaos and clarity in trading lies not in external circumstances but in internal mastery. This chapter will explore the final lessons from both traders' paths, reinforcing the core message: success in trading is a journey of mastering oneself.

The Diverging Paths of Chaos and Clarity

Let us look back at the stories of Lashwik, the Clarity Trader, and Durwin, the Chaos Trader.

Both started at the same point, eager and full of ambition to conquer the markets. They had access to the same tools, similar knowledge of trading strategies, and equal opportunities. However, their journeys took dramatically different turns. Why? The answer lies in their approach to the most important aspect of trading—controlling their mindset and emotions.

Durwin, the Chaos Trader, represents the trader who allows emotions to dominate his decision-making. His trading is driven by fear, greed, and doubt, and as a result, his experience is a rollercoaster of inconsistent wins and heavy losses. After every setback, Durwin changes his strategy, hoping that the next one will finally lead to lasting success. But he never pauses to realize that the problem isn't in the strategies he chooses—it's in his inability to control his emotions. Every loss becomes a reason for panic; every win fuels overconfidence. He remains stuck in the loop of emotional trading, forever searching for the magic formula that will make everything perfect.

In contrast, Lashwik, the Clarity Trader, approaches trading with a sense of calm. He doesn't just rely on strategies—he combines them with disciplined habits and emotional control. Instead of reacting emotionally to the market's volatility, he trusts his process. He understands that losses are a part of the game and that success is measured over the long run, not by short-term gains. His belief in himself, combined with the ability to visualize his success, creates an unshakable foundation for his trading journey.

What makes Lashwik successful isn't that he never experiences losses; it's that he never lets those losses define him. He learns from them, adjusts his process if needed, but remains steady in his belief that as long as he maintains discipline, the results will follow.

The Importance of Emotional Mastery

The key difference between the two traders was not knowledge or market conditions—it was emotional mastery.

Trading is an inherently emotional activity. When money is on the line, especially hard-earned money, the stakes feel high. It's easy to feel elated after a big win or devastated after a loss. But those who succeed in trading understand that these emotions must be managed, not indulged.

Lashwik's mentor once told him, "The market doesn't care about your feelings. It only reacts to your actions." This simple truth became a guiding principle in his trading. He learned to separate his emotions from his actions. When the market moved against him, he didn't panic; he followed his plan. When he experienced a winning streak, he didn't get cocky; he stayed grounded. In mastering his emotions,

Lashwik learned to see the market for what it was—a neutral environment that responds only to logic and discipline, not fear or excitement.

Durwin, however, was never able to break free from the grip of his emotions. His fear of losing led him to make rash decisions, while his greed caused him to overtrade. Even when he won, he was constantly anxious, fearing that his luck would run out. Without emotional mastery, he was always a step behind, reacting instead of proactively following a plan.

Belief and Visualization: The Inner Edge

One of the most powerful tools Lashwik had on his journey was his ability to believe in his success long before it materialized. As we discussed earlier in this book, belief is the foundation for success—not just in trading, but in life. By focusing on positive outcomes and visualizing himself as a disciplined and successful trader, Lashwik created a mental image that became his reality.

This concept, inspired by teachings from *The Secret*, suggests that what you focus on is what you attract. If you constantly focus on fear and failure, as Durwin did, you will invite those experiences into your life. But if you focus on discipline, consistency, and success, as Lashwik did, those things will become part of your journey.

Visualization was a daily practice for Lashwik. Every morning before the market opened, he would take time to visualize his ideal trading day. He wouldn't just imagine making profits—he would see himself following his strategy, making calm, informed decisions, and accepting losses with grace. By doing this, Lashwik conditioned his mind to behave in that way when the time came to trade.

Durwin, however, allowed his mind to be filled with doubt and negativity. He feared losses, obsessed over bad trades, and constantly replayed his mistakes in his head. This negative focus prevented him from achieving clarity, keeping him trapped in the same patterns of emotional trading.

Trusting the Process

Another important distinction between Lashwik and Durwin was their focus. Lashwik was committed to the process of trading, while Durwin was obsessed with the outcome of each individual trade. This difference may seem subtle, but it is what separates consistent traders from erratic ones.

Lashwik understood that he couldn't control the outcome of every trade. Some trades would be winners, others would be losers. But as long as he followed his strategy and remained disciplined, the overall results would take care of themselves. He trusted that the process would yield profits over time, even if there were setbacks along the way.

Durwin, however, lived trade-to-trade. Every time he lost, he doubted his process and looked for a new strategy. Every time he won, he overestimated his skills and took unnecessary risks. By focusing only on short-term outcomes, Durwin never developed the long-term consistency that Lashwik achieved.

The Path to Mastery

At the heart of this journey is the concept of mastery—both in trading and in oneself. For Lashwik, mastery didn't come from memorizing strategies or learning every technical indicator; it came from mastering his emotions, his mindset, and his discipline. This mastery allowed him to enter "the zone," where trading felt effortless and intuitive.

Durwin, despite his best efforts, never reached this level of mastery. He remained stuck in the early stages of his journey, constantly reacting to external events instead of mastering his inner world.

But here's the most important takeaway: the path to clarity is available to everyone. Lashwik wasn't born with these skills; he developed them through practice, reflection, and the guidance of a mentor. Similarly, Durwin's story could have been different had he chosen to focus on emotional mastery and process-oriented thinking.

Final Thoughts: Your Journey to Clarity

As we conclude this book, remember that trading success is not defined by how much money you make or how many strategies you learn. It is defined by your ability to master yourself. The lessons from Lashwik's journey are available to anyone willing to put in the effort:

1. **Embrace Emotional Mastery**: Learn to recognize and control your emotions while trading. Don't let fear or greed drive your decisions.
2. **Focus on Process, Not Outcomes**: Trust your strategy, follow your process, and don't get caught up in the results of individual trades.
3. **Believe in Your Success**: Adopt a positive mindset and visualize yourself as a disciplined, successful trader. This mental practice will shape your reality.
4. **Stay Consistent**: Trading is a marathon, not a sprint. Success comes from small, disciplined actions over time.

Your journey to clarity in trading begins now. Just like Lashwik, you have the ability to transform chaos into consistent success, but it starts with mastering your mind and emotions. Trust the process, focus on self-discipline, and, above all, believe in your capacity to succeed.

The journey from chaos to clarity is one of personal growth and transformation. As you continue your trading journey, remember that it's not the market you must conquer—it's yourself.